CATHOLIC PENTECOSTALS

CATHOLIC PENTECOSTALS

by

Kevin and Dorothy Ranaghan

PAULIST PRESS DEUS BOOKS

Paramus, N.J.   New York, N.Y.

Toronto, Ont.

ACKNOWLEDGMENTS

The authors would like to thank *The National Catholic Reporter* for permission to quote from "People Having a Good Time Praying" by Mary Papa; Bernard Geis Associates for permission to quote from *The Cross and the Switchblade,* © 1963 by David Wilkerson; Harcourt, Brace & World for permission to quote from *The Third Revolution* by Karl Stern; The McGraw-Hill Book Co. for permission to quote from *They Speak With Other Tongues* by John L. Sherrill, © 1964; and Helicon Press, Inc., for permission to reprint Joseph Connelly's translation of the Sequence from Pentecost which appeared in the *Layman's Missal.*

Published by Paulist Press
Editorial Office: 1865 Broadway, N.Y., N.Y. 10023
Business Office: Paramus, New Jersey 07652

Printed and bound in the
United States of America
by Our Sunday Visitor Press

Contents

INTRODUCTION 1

1 Stirrings in Pittsburgh 6

  Bearing Witness 24

2 Growth at Notre Dame 38

  Bearing Witness 58

3 Roots of the Baptism in the Holy Spirit 107

4 Pentecostal Experience Today 141

5 The Gifts and Fruit of the Spirit 157

6 Speaking in Tongues 191

7 Walking in the Spirit 209

APPENDIX I: PENTECOSTALISM IN
  HISTORICAL PERSPECTIVE 249

APPENDIX II: TOWARD A THEOLOGY
  OF PENTECOSTALISM 259

SUGGESTED READING 263

A New Pentecost

May there be repeated thus in the Christian families the spectacle of the apostles gathered together in Jerusalem after the Ascension of Jesus to heaven, when the newborn Church was completely united in communion of thought and prayer with Peter and around Peter, the shepherd of the lambs and of the sheep. And may the Divine Spirit deign to answer in a most comforting manner the prayer that rises daily to Him from every corner of the earth: "Renew your wonders in our time, as though for a new Pentecost, and grant that the holy Church, preserving unanimous and continuous prayer, together with Mary, the mother of Jesus, and also under the guidance of Saint Peter, may increase the reign of the Divine Savior, the reign of truth and justice, the reign of love and peace. Amen."

POPE JOHN XXIII
Humanae Salutis

Introduction

Friday nights being what they are on this all-male campus, many of the students who wandered into the prayer meeting were just sightseeing. They had read that some of their classmates and professors were doing strange things such as "speaking in tongues" and driving out devils.

You could tell the sightseers. They wore "show-me" smirks. As knowledge of the pentecostal prayer meetings at Notre Dame spread, so did misunderstanding.

To many it seemed incongruous that a movement previously associated with lower class Protestantism and fundamentalism should take root in a Catholic university ablaze with the progressive light of the Vatican Council.

In this context, the bizarre elements of the pentecostal meetings became the focus of both curiosity and downright concern.

The National Catholic Reporter (May 17, 1967)

In Room 316 of the Administration Building of Notre Dame University sat a typical group of college people: undergrads, coeds from St. Mary's College, faculty members, a few priests and sisters, and a smattering of lay people from the city. Thirty, maybe forty, people gathered in a classroom for an evening is a very normal thing. But there was something abnormal in this group. They all professed the belief that Jesus Christ was present in the room, and that the Holy Spirit was there, too—moving in them and

1

speaking through them. Over to one side a girl spoke of how a friend had introduced her to Jesus. In the center a man related how a week before a sister had been cured of a long-standing back ailment when a prayer group asked Jesus to take care of it. Still another young woman announced a "message from God," speaking in the first person. As if this were not disconcerting enough to anyone who happened to pass the wide-open doors, every once in a while an individual or the group as a whole started to talk in a burst of foreign language, or at least foreign sounds which nobody understood. If you asked one of them what he was doing, he would respond with a certain joy, "Oh, we are praying in tongues; you know, praising God in languages we never learned but which the Holy Spirit gave us."

This scene, strange and disturbing as it may seem, is now taking place regularly in dozens of American cities and towns, not only on campuses, but in church basements, convents, monasteries, and private homes. The participants in these meetings, which stretch from one end of the country to another, seem otherwise to be normal, healthy people, well-balanced, involved in many things including a full and active life in the Catholic Church. They are involved in what is being called the Catholic pentecostal movement, and they number in the thousands.

The American Catholic is fast becoming accustomed to rapid changes in his Church. Renewal is the word most often heard these days as age-old customs once held sacrosanct pass from the realm of religious practice into history. In the aftermath of Vatican II, with its emphasis on the development of committed Christian personality in a vital Christian community, we see the regulation of fasting give way to personal responsibility, medieval and baroque attitudes on the Mass and sacraments yield to relevant adaptation and experimentation for today's worshipping assembly. The Church declares that it must serve the world and all people in it. The news media are filled with accounts of priests and religious deeply involved in the issues of civil rights and social justice. Formerly, the Gospel was preached in the churches; now, it seems, it is to be acted out in the inner city. For ours is an age of movements: the liturgical movement, the civil rights movement, the scriptural movement, the peace movement, the ecumenical movement. On every side we see signs of the People of God striving to renew themselves in Christ, to be the community Christ wanted, and to show forth Christ effectively in the modern world. Our Church is changing; it is growing, and the growing pains are felt by all of us.

This is the story of still another movement. For us it began stirring around 1966; yet, in a very real sense it is as old as Christianity, rooted in its foundation. In one respect it is like other movements, involving people, projects and progress. Yet, since it is unlike any purely human effort we have ever witnessed, it is seen as a genuine movement of Christ in his Church renewing his mystical body. It has been called the "pentecostal movement." It is essentially a movement of faith and prayer; faith in Jesus Christ, and confident prayer that he will fulfill in us and through us his plan for the world. In our age "God is dead." He is thought dead because he is "missing in action." The Christian looks within and around himself and sees only sin and weakness, an ineffective apostolate, and he hears only the pounding roar of God's silence.

He looks to scripture and sees what appears to be only the records of past prophets and past deeds which, though powerful, do not speak to him. Satellites, computers, and psychologists give us the answers to most of life's former riddles. It would seem that the God who was merely a crutch is indeed dead. To this age of questioning, God has sent his prophets and his signs and wonders to call to men, "I, the Lord am with you." So that today's Church may be as vibrant as the apostolic Church, so that today's Christian may be as open to the will of the Father as was that early band of disciples, so that the power of Christ might penetrate the disbelief, the Christians involved in this "movement" seek the continued outpouring of Christ's Spirit, the Holy Spirit.

The results have been truly astonishing. Put together, the accounts would read like a section of the Acts of the Apostles. But stated briefly, hundreds of Catholics have had their prayers for renewal answered in a most remarkable and dramatic transformation of their lives. Many who were committed Christians at work for Christ in his Church have experienced their lives in Christ considerably deepened. Others, on the fringe of Christianity, or grown cool in the faith, have been remarkably transformed into full, active believers. Some, Catholic in name only who had abandoned Christ completely, have turned to him genuinely and have begun to walk in faith. Results of the "pentecostal movement" might be summed up as one typically 20th century student expressed it: "It works!"

Belief that God would act with power in our day began as a spark in Pittsburgh, Pennsylvania in the fall of 1966, and by the power of the Holy Spirit it has become a raging flame; from east to west it continues to spread the word that God is alive, that Jesus lives and walks and speaks to us now, that he is true to his promises, that he is truly Emmanuel—God with us! The story that we tell here is that from the embers of the Christian past we are witness now to the fire of a new Pentecost.

1

Stirrings in Pittsburgh

> One weekend ... the Ranaghans entertained
> friends from Duquesne University in Pittsburgh.
> Their friends described pentecostal experiences
> they had been a part of in Pittsburgh.
>
> *The National Catholic Reporter*

Perched atop one of the many hills which form
the center of the city of Pittsburgh is a cluster of
buildings—and a community of faculty and students
which make up Duquesne University of the Holy
Spirit. It is windy on the hill; a strong breeze from
the river whips the legs of coeds and wildly tosses
hair around, especially in the fall. In the fall the poet
and the mystic among us could sense in the very air
the Spirit who comes with the "violent wind" and
who "blows where he will."

In the fall of 1966 several Catholic laymen, all
members of the faculty of Duquesne University in
Pittsburgh were drawn together in a period of deep
prayer and discussion about the vitality of their faith
life. These men had been committed to Christ for a
number of years and were involved in a number of
apostolic activities. Not satisfied with a life of ivory
tower scholarship, they concerned themselves with the
problems of renewal in the Church. Growing pains of
the Church were very much a part of their daily
existence. In recent years they had been involved with

the liturgical and ecumenical movements, with civil rights, and with the concerns of world peace. These were men of prayer whose lives were centered on the worship of our Father in and through Jesus Christ.

In spite of all this they felt there was something lacking in their individual Christian lives. They couldn't quite put their fingers on it but somehow there was an emptiness, a lack of dynamism, a sapping of strength in their lives of prayer and action. It was as if their lives as Christians were too much their own creation, as if they were moving forward under their own power and out of their own will. It seemed to them that the Christian life wasn't meant to be a purely human achievement. The Christian is part of Christ's Church, his body extended throughout history, and the power source of this Christian should be the redeeming love of the risen Jesus. For Christianity is not the following of a certain philosopher; it is the actual sharing in the life and love of God. For some reason that dynamism of the risen Lord, that pervading awareness of living in him, here and now, was missing. If we do live in Christ, and if Christ is really present in the Church—and through the Church present to the world—it is because after his ascension to the right hand of the Father, he sent his Holy Spirit upon the first Christian community. This is the mystery of Pentecost, the birthday of the Church.

In an instant the band of disciples was transformed into a community of faith and love. Without shame or fear they praised God and witnessed to the mystery of Jesus. They picked up and continued his work, they conveyed the Father's love to sinners, preached repentance and salvation in Jesus, and in his name they healed the sick just as he had done. They became

strong and confident in prayer, continuing the celebration of Christ's death and resurrection in the
eucharistic banquet. By what power did they do all
this? They were filled with the Holy Spirit, just as
Jesus had promised. Yes, Jesus had left them and returned to the Father; but he had not left them
orphans. Instead, he sent his Spirit upon them to
make himself present in the world. An overwhelming
awareness of Jesus' presence in their midst, and a
boldness and confidence as his missionaries—this was
the work of the Holy Spirit on the disciples at
Pentecost.

Realizing this, these men in Pittsburgh began to
pray that the Holy Spirit of Christ would renew in
them all the graces of their baptism and confirmation,
that he would fill up in them the vacuum left by
human effort with the powerful life of the risen Lord.
Each day they prayed for each other the "Come Holy
Spirit"—the sequence for the liturgy of Pentecost
Sunday. As they prayed, they began to study the New
Testament again, particularly the sections dealing
with the life of the primitive Church, and they poured
over the history of the early Church. Slowly the answer became clear. When the early Christians sought
the fullness of Christian life, they prayed with genuine
confidence and expectation that Christ's Spirit would
come upon them, and invariably he did come. He
came in a way that transformed former life into a
life suffused with Christ's love, into a life whose every
breath was a prayer of praise, whose every deed was
an act of faith, whose every word cried out for all to
hear: "Jesus is Lord." And so they began to expect
that the Holy Spirit would come upon them in the
same way. Expectation gave way to events.

It was during the National Cursillo Convention, in August of 1966, that they were casually introduced to a book which opened the door to a new world for them. They met some friends, Steve Clark and Ralph Martin, who at that time were staff members of Saint John's Student Parish in East Lansing, Michigan. Steve had been reading a book which intrigued yet puzzled him. He didn't quite know what to make of it and he urged them to read it.

The Cross and the Switchblade is the account of the life and spiritual adventures of David Wilkerson as edited and written by John Sherrill. It is the story of Wilkerson's powerful Christian service among young gang members and dope addicts in the Bedford-Stuyvesant section of New York City. The men from Pittsburgh read the book when they returned from the convention. One of them decided to check it against the bible. The latter part of the book is particularly concerned with the gift of the Holy Spirit, "baptism in the Spirit," the whole role of the Holy Spirit in the life of the Christian, how Jesus is the true "baptizer" in the Holy Spirit, and how the baptism is received. It contained many scriptural references. He sat down with the bible, turned particularly to Luke's gospel and Acts and started to read. As he put it: "I then began to flip like mad all through the bible, particularly through the New Testament, and found, for four solid hours, that the whole bible was opened to me in a way it had never been before. I don't think I moved from my chair." Wilkerson's book was a kind of lead into scriptural doctrine. Their eyes were opened to many texts which they had seen before, dozens and dozens of times, yet had never been quite able to put together.

These texts said clearly that the culmination of Christ's messianic career was the fact that just as he had received the Spirit to be messiah and Lord, and that this was the key to his whole personality and role and mission in life, so it was his great gift to his disciples. They would not be his disciples, they could not be Christians in any sense of the word unless they were anointed, unless they were christened, unless they had received the Spirit as he had. Then they could live and walk as his disciples. It seemed so clear, so compelling, so overwhelming. It was almost like discovering Christianity for the first time. The book spoke of the indwelling and powerful Spirit as the motive and moving power of our Christian lives. It was very old doctrine, it was very traditional doctrine, it was a very Catholic doctrine, yet it was filled with a kind of newness of discovery and insight, deepening through the testimony of Christians who were right now living under the influence of this power. In their struggles with the apathy and unbelief among college students they realized they needed the kind of power that Wilkerson seemed to possess in the face of the agony and ugliness of the dropouts, delinquents and addicts of Brooklyn. They shared, read and talked and prayed about the book for the next two months.

During that time, in an attempt to deal with, and deepen their formation of, Christian attitudes and practices, these men in Pittsburgh had been praying for one another consistently, all year, every day, the famous and beautiful "golden sequence" as it is called, a hymn to the Holy Spirit which is used in the Mass during the week of Pentecost. During this same time, one of the men, Ralph Keifer, an instructor in the theology department at Duquesne, had been led to read another book by John Sherrill entitled *They Speak With Other Tongues.* The book contained a powerful and persuasive analysis of pentecostalism in this country which Ralph enthusiastically recounted to the others. They were now faced with some practical possibilities. Ralph enumerated them. He was convinced that they had prayed enough, had thought enough and that they should probably get to meet somebody, some live Christian in the flesh who had had these experiences, and to talk about it directly. Yet, he proposed some alternatives. One was that they could go on praying, talking about it, and maybe something would happen, something would turn up. They sort of discarded that. (It didn't seem to be very promising because they had been doing that for some time without having the experience which was recounted in those books and which seemed to be so apparent in the Acts of the Apostles.) Secondly, they could with faith and confidence pray for and lay hands on each other in an attempt to follow the pattern found in scripture. This seemed like a kind of spiritual turning in on one another, and they thought it wasn't the best way. Perhaps, after all, it seemed they should go to somebody else. The only thing they could think of was some pentecostal church. They had some scruples about this, however, because, as one of them put it, "I had a little experience with certain forms of pentecostal churches and they didn't exactly suit my Anglo-Saxon temperament. Besides, I didn't exactly know any live pentecostal and I couldn't just walk up to one and say 'Can I come to your church?'" Ralph, who had some experience with pentecostals when he was very young, thought they were rather wild and wooly and that they had a long tradition of possibly anti-Catholic sentiments which, however understandable, might provoke more discussion than spiritual fellowship. What to do next?

While groping around they suddenly remembered an Episcopalian priest who had come to Duquesne once to lecture to a group of students. He seemed like a very fine man, well-informed, well-read, well-balanced and so forth. As a kind of long shot, a call was placed to the Episcopalian chancery in downtown Pittsburgh. They asked where William Lewis was. They found out he was the rector of a large Episcopalian parish, Christ Church, in the North Hills of Pittsburgh, so they called him up and asked him if he'd ever heard of Wilkerson's or Sherrill's books. He said "Yes, as I'm sitting here in my chair I can see them right on my bookshelf. Some friends of mine in the parish gave them to me . . . Yes, I have read them . . . Yes, I found them very interesting. No, I don't quite know what to make of them . . . but I'm very interested." When Keifer and his friends asked whether he had such a prayer group in his parish, he said, "Well, that's another interesting question. As I look out my window I can see a lady's house where a prayer group of that kind meets every Friday night." They pursued the question further. The upshot of it was that Mr. Lewis said he would put them into contact with a parishioner, an Episcopalian lady named Betty Schomaker whom he described as a member in very good standing in his parish, a very fine woman whom he admired very much, an excellent Christian, and a permanent member of a pentecostal prayer group. He said she would probably be a little shy about advertising the fact, that they were not giving publicity or too much public discussion to it, but he was sure if he reassured her as to their sincerity that she would be glad to meet with them.

It turned out that the upcoming Christmas holidays were not very practical for such a meeting. But on Friday, January 6, they met in Mr. Lewis' office in the church building. He not only introduced them to Mrs. Schomaker, but he joined in on the discussion, shared his thoughts and helped everyone to pool their mutual knowledge, interest and experience. It does not seem incidental that January 6 is the feast of the Epiphany, the manifestation of Jesus Christ as Son of God, as one baptized by the Holy Spirit and the one who baptizes in the Holy Spirit. It turned out to be a quiet yet momentous morning. Mrs. Schomaker was, in their estimation, eminently a lady, well-educated, not the least bit excitable, not the least bit interested in intriguing them with her experiences. They found her to be forthright, simple, direct, and scriptural. She did confirm what they knew from the books, told them about their prayer meeting, and after she had discovered that they were sincere seekers of God and his will, she invited them to come the following Friday.

January 13 is the octave day of the Epiphany, set aside in Catholic liturgy to celebrate the baptism of Jesus in the Jordan River by the Holy Spirit. On this day they met at the home of Miss Florence Dodge, a Presbyterian who had organized the prayer group some time previously. It was held regularly at her house, and she was a quasi-leader of the meetings. She was a well-educated woman, with a responsible position in a large Pittsburgh department store. She had taught Sunday school and adult education classes and had a well-rounded background. Aside from Mrs.

Schomaker, they did not know anyone at this meeting when they arrived. Ralph Keifer gave the following impressions of this first meeting and of the events which followed.

"My wife, two colleagues and I walked cautiously into a 'pure suburbia' home and were immediately struck by the warmth of the people there. It was like a family gathering, and we belonged. I remember that they sang four or five traditional mainline Protestant Sunday school type hymns to open the meeting. A lengthy spontaneous prayer session followed. There was one person leading out at a time, and while it was certainly not babble there was an undertone of voices, and a little praying in tongues. This, too, was done quite softly and unobtrusively. They then began to share biblical passages in a most remarkable way. They shared what they had read in the last week and related it to a variety of experiences both past and present. What startled us about this is that the theology of Christian life which emerged was excellent. It was a resurrection-oriented grace theology of the kind usually found in cursillos and in good textbooks in theology; yet, it was neither contrived nor from a textbook. The operative theology of the group as it met and prayed together was positive, natural, and joyful, since it was grounded in the Pauline epistles. I winced once or twice when someone mentioned intelligence and how 'dangerous it is, etc.' In fact, I was about to start grinding my teeth till someone said, 'You know, I think the Lord means to use that too . . .' and this began a very positive discussion. My only other objection seemed to center on the way they were using scripture. Fundamentalist is not the right word. It was much more that they were tending to read the scriptures like the Fathers of the Church did, in a highly allegorical manner. It put me off for a while. But even through this I could see a real testimony of the sense of the presence of God. Maybe that's why it bothered me. I fear a 'super-direct pipeline to God' mentality. Yet, as one of my friends said after the meeting, maybe we overemphasize secondary causality too much so that we never have a sense of God working in anything. In all it was not an extraordinary evening. Yet, it led us to think and to pray. We were left with an abiding sense that here was a movement of God.

"Of the four of us who attended this first meeting, for a number of reasons only Patrick Bourgeois, a fellow instructor in the theology department, and I were able to make it to the next meeting. We returned to find the prayer and discussion centered this time upon the Epistle to the Romans. The only way I can express the way we felt about this discussion was that it was not all clouded up by Reformation issues. They weren't saying anything that I felt to be a problem. It was a strikingly nondenominational meeting. It ended when Pat and I asked to be prayed with for the baptism in the Holy Spirit. They broke up into several groups because they were praying over several people. They simply asked me to make an act of faith for the power of the Spirit to work in me. I prayed in tongues rather quickly. It was not a particularly soaring or spectacular thing at all. I felt a certain peace—and at least a little prayerful—and truthfully, rather curious as to where all this would lead. They broke out food afterwards and had a little party. I remember that my comment to them that night was 'see what you do when you have Catholics here, you

have rites and ceremonies.' They had never done that
before. They had always sort of just broken up and
gone home. That night, however, was a sort of celebration.

"To me, praying in tongues was a rather minimal
aspect, a purely concomitant phenomenon which
seemed naturally to go along with this. I was interested in it mainly because I felt my faith needed
'livening.' That was the prime concern—speaking in
tongues didn't really present an intellectual problem
because I knew historically that it had been a phenomenon which was widely accepted in the Church in
its beginning. And from what I knew of Church history the New Testament phenomenon was not limited
to the New Testament by any means. My personal
difficulty had been the reverse. I couldn't understand
why this charismatic phenomenon didn't occur more
frequently, as one would expect. This seemed to be
more in line with what I had come to expect of New
Testament Christianity."

In the following week, Ralph laid hands on the
two others, and they too, received the baptism in the
Holy Spirit. One of them summed up the difference
it made in this way:

"Talk about a baptism, it was just like I was
being plunged down into a great sea of water, only the
water was God, the water was the Holy Spirit . . . All
in all it is not a new experience. It is not a revolutionary experience because it reaffirmed all the things
which I'd been trying to hold on to for years and to
affirm for so many years: my appreciation of scripture,
my appreciation of the eucharist, my appreciation of
praying and working with other people. The difference is that it seems to me that everything is easier

and more spontaneous and comes from within. It is not so much that I am trying to pray or that I am trying to work with people or that I am trying to advert to God or to pay attention to him, to make him the center of my life. This seems to be now a much more spontaneous welling up of these aspirations and this power from within. This is not saying that I've overcome all my difficulties, not by a long shot, it's just that there's more inwardness and spontaneity, more power in a word than there ever was before.

"And this has lasted and endured. It can be lessened or weakened by lack of faith because I am sure that God doesn't work despite us. We have to cooperate with him and let him act, let him have his own way because there is nothing automatic, nothing mechanical, nothing magical, nothing superstitious about it. It is still the old-fashioned Christian life which was first taught to me when I was a child, and yet it has a certain new dimension, a new strength and a new power and interiority which it did not have before, for which I thank him with my whole heart."

The instrument which the Lord used to answer this prayer in faith for renewal is called the "baptism in the Holy Spirit." This phrase found in the Acts of the Apostles describes the action of Christians praying together for the coming of the Holy Spirit. As you have seen, when the people in Pittsburgh describe their experience with the "baptism in the Holy Spirit" they talk of a new awareness of the love of God, particularly as it is offered to them through the risen Christ. Jesus became familiar to them in a new way, and they were at ease in approaching him as Lord and as brother, so conscious were they of his nearness.

Their prayers turned spontaneously to praise of God, and the desire to pray increased in them.

Suddenly the bible had a new attraction for them. Long-time students of scripture, they began to read the Old and New Testaments for sheer joy and to rejoice in the wonderful things the Father has done throughout salvation history. They were at peace in a remarkable way. Serious problems of personality, of tensions between individuals, of work or of study, worked themselves out with ease in the context of the love of Christ. A new faith filled them. Not only were they more fully committed to Christ, but they found a new boldness in faith, a confidence in Christ's presence and loving power that enabled them to speak out about Christ to friends without embarassment. And on all sides, even in trial, they attested to the pervading joy that accompanied this more intense life with Christ.

Along with this marvellous interior transformation, they received many or all of the gifts of the Holy Spirit. These are the charisms found in the early Church in great abundance. Then, they were given by the Spirit to Christians to serve the community, to build up its faith, and to manifest the loving presence of Christ. These gifts of the Holy Spirit detailed in 1 Corinthians 12, once thought to belong only to the early Church, were being received with joy by members of the 20th-century American Catholic Church. Here were the higher gifts of speaking with wisdom and with understanding, discernment of the influences of good and evil spirits, prophecy, spiritual and physical healing. Things we have read about, works of God we believed in—for the early Church— these things which we thought had no place in today's technological society now were present and becoming part of normal Christian experience.

There is another gift that they received. It seems very strange. Although St. Paul reminds us that it is certainly not the most important of the gifts of the Holy Spirit, yet it continues to attract the most attention wherever the pentecostal movement is discussed. This is called the gift of tongues. It may be described as the praising of God in a new language, a language which the speaker does not understand, yet which he himself speaks. Very often at the baptism in the Holy Spirit the recipient is moved to speak out certain sounds or syllables which are strange. When one yields fully to this impulse, he finds himself in an attitude of intense prayer, but praying in a strange tongue. Usually the prayer is unintelligible, yet it has a pattern, a vocabulary, a series of inflections which indicate true human speech. St. Paul tells us that on such occasions the Spirit prays within us, knowing how and what to pray better than we ever could.

Many and various studies have been made on this subject. We will discuss it in more detail in chapter 6. But for the moment what we wish to stress is that the phenomenon of praising God in strange languages as the disciples did on Pentecost, as the early Christians of Corinth did, and as other Christians have done throughout the history of the Church, very often accompanies "baptism in the Holy Spirit." While it is called the least of the gifts, it is often but not always the first received. For many it is thus a threshold through which one passes into the realm of the gifts and fruits of the Holy Spirit—gifts, which serve to conform the Christian more closely to Christ and to serve the needs of the community of Christians.

Seen as a manifestation of the presence of the Holy Spirit, the gift of tongues is a very beautiful thing. And since it often presages a new stage in the development of Christian personality, it seems a good thing to desire and pray for.

By February of 1967, the four Catholics from Pittsburgh had received baptism in the Holy Spirit. In great joy they began to witness quietly among close friends about what the Lord had done for them. Doctrinally they could see no problem with it. It is definitely scriptural. Further, it was in no way considered a sacrament of the Church, much less a replacement for the sacraments. On the contrary, everyone experienced a greater desire for participation in the sacramental life of the Church than before. "Baptism in the Holy Spirit" is not something replacing baptism and confirmation. Rather it may be seen as an adult re-affirmation and renewal of these sacraments, an opening of ourselves to all their sacramental graces. The gesture of the "laying on of hands" which often accompanies "baptism in the Holy Spirit" is not a new sacramental rite. It is a fraternal gesture of love and concern, a visible sign of human corporeality so necessary for any fully human religious experience. The spontaneous prayer of the "baptism in the Holy Spirit" is prayer in utter faith and expectation that the Holy Spirit will come upon the individual as Jesus wants him to come. Nothing was contradictory to the teaching of the Church; on the other hand, the results of "baptism in the Holy Spirit" seemed to be greatly desired by all Christians, establishing as they do a closer union with Christ.

In mid-February a small group of students together with the faculty members from Duquesne decided to spend a weekend in prayer, meditating over the first four chapters of the Acts of the Apostles and seeking the will of God. About thirty people made this retreat. On the whole the students knew little if anything of "baptism in the Holy Spirit" or of the gifts and fruits of the Spirit as they had been recently manifest; nor were the faculty members trying to steer them toward this experience. The majority of the students in preparation for the weekend had read David Wilkerson's book, *The Cross and the Switchblade,* which talks so powerfully of the action of God in the lives of young people. All then simply gathered together in prayer to seek the will of Jesus Christ for their lives.

This "Duquesne weekend" as it has come to be called was certainly one of the most remarkable incidents in the story of the pentecostal movement. Although there have been many similar stories from around the world, this was an outstanding example of the swift gracious action of the Holy Spirit toward those who are open to him.

All day Saturday the group met for prayer and study. Saturday evening had been set aside for relaxation. As a matter of fact, it was to have been a large birthday party for one of the priests who was on the retreat. As one girl put it, "We were tired of praying, and we weren't going to spend the evening in prayer, too."

One engaged couple, Paul Grey and Maryanne Springle, had heard about the "baptism in the Holy Spirit" and they desired it. So they approached Ralph Keifer and asked him to pray with them that the Holy Spirit would become fully active in their lives. Quietly they slipped upstairs, away from the crowd, and there, in prayer, they were deeply touched by the Spirit of Christ. The Spirit soon manifested himself in the gift of tongues with which the young man and woman praised God. After some time they decided to return to the group below but not to tell what happened to them.

What they did not know was that simultaneously one of the girls, a Duquesne coed, Patti Gallagher, had felt drawn to the chapel, and there had felt the almost tangible presence of the Spirit of Christ. In awe she left the chapel and quickly urged others in the building to join her there. By ones and twos the small group made their way to the chapel. And as they were gathered together there in prayer, the Holy Spirit poured himself out upon them.

There was no urging, there was no direction as to what had to be done. The individuals simply encountered the person of the Holy Spirit as others had several weeks before. Some praised God in new languages, others quietly wept for joy, others prayed and sang. They prayed from ten in the evening until five in the morning. Not everyone was touched immediately, but throughout the evening God dealt with each person there in a wonderful way.

What is more important, and from a certain point of view more impressive, is the reception of the fruits of the Holy Spirit which this group experienced. The hours of near physical experience of the Lord touched many; they have been followed by months of living closer to Christ, of sharing the peace, joy, love, and confident faith described above. In the ensuing weeks the Lord touched many others through this group; some turned from lives of sin; others from intellectual doubt turned and embraced the Lord Jesus in mature acts of faith. Throughout the remainder of the spring semester at Duquesne the external gifts and the internal fruits (if we may make such a division) of the Holy Spirit continued to be poured out in this little community of faith and spread the joy of Christ's love to many Catholics in the university area. And it has lasted.

The four testimonies in the following section are but an indication of the various ways in which the Lord dealt with each one in that weekend of renewal and revival.

BEARING WITNESS

David Mangan

*David Mangan received his B.A. from Duquesne
University. He is presently teaching mathematics
and religion at St. Thomas High School in Brad-
dock, Pennsylvania.*

On February 17, 1967, I hurried home from work
with a new four-track stereo tape recorder I had just
bought. I really wanted to use it and learn about it
badly. But for some strange reason I left it untouched
and prepared to leave for the weekend to make a
retreat with some friends from Duquesne University.
Several times I had attempted to give myself excuses for not going, but each time my excuses were
refuted and I was spurred on.

The main theme of the weekend was the Holy
Spirit. We had been asked to read *The Cross and the
Switchblade* and the first four chapters of the Acts
of the Apostles as a preparation. The strange thing
was that I had planned to teach a lesson on the
Holy Spirit to my religion class. I decided against
it because I felt I did not know enough about it
myself. Now I figured this would be my chance to
learn.

On Saturday morning we had a talk on the first
chapter of Acts. The main points were that the
Spirit means power and that one must have a total

dependence on the Spirit. The role of prayer was
emphasized. I accepted these things with the usual
fervor, not realizing the extent of the message.
We broke up into discussion groups and talked
about this. My question was, "Is the Spirit *really*
powerful?" The answer given to me by someone I
truly respect was "Yes." Just a plain and simple yes.
I didn't even get a supporting argument. But I
believed him and I prayed that I could receive this
power.

In the afternoon we had a talk on the second
chapter of Acts. This talk emphasized how to go about
receiving this power . . . A few personal instances
were recounted about people speaking in tongues,
but I must admit I still didn't realize what was
meant. My reaction to this was that I wrote in my
notebook: "I want to hear someone speak in tongues
—me."

We again broke up into discussion groups.
The result of this one was that I realized what my
reception of the Holy Spirit in the sacrament of
confirmation was supposed to be and how I didn't
participate in it. So along with a friend I decided
to do something to renew or take up what I did at
confirmation. We were then dismissed, and my friend
and I walked together discussing what we had
heard and what we had decided. Upon returning to
the house we received some startling news—we had
no supply of water. Either the spring had dried up
or the pump had broken, but we had no water.
There were about five of us in the room and one of
the leaders of the weekend asked us what we were
going to do about it. Our reaction was, "We can't
do anything!" Then he suggested that we pray. At

that time I really felt stupid. I felt like the apostles must have felt when they would make a dumb remark after being around Jesus. We collected some others and prayed. We became so sure that it was not God's will for us to go home yet that we prayed in thanksgiving for the water he was going to give us so we could stay.

After we finished praying we went back to the normal course of events and expected results. In the early evening we had a bible vigil which was to be followed by a birthday party for three people present. About five minutes before the bible vigil I was really struck with the realization that I was going to go downstairs and see the water. So immediately afterward I went down into the kitchen and turned on the water. It was there with even more force than usual. What really surprised me was that I didn't even get excited. I just said to myself, "Of course, it's here, why shouldn't it be?" I walked out into the hall and announced that we had water. Those who had prayed with me (some didn't even know the water was gone) were really joyful. I then continued upstairs and told some more people outside the chapel, and before I knew it I was walking into the chapel. I stood before the altar and the next thing I knew I was lying prostrate on the floor crying and feeling such ecstasy as I may never feel again. I cried harder than I ever cried in my life, but I did not shed one tear. All of a sudden Jesus Christ was so real and so present that I could feel him all around. I was overcome with such a feeling of love that I cannot begin to describe it.

After a period of time (I don't know how long) I was helped to my feet and went downstairs knowing

that the Spirit of God had just dealt with me. As
I walked downstairs I could see only love on faces,
and I was not aware of anything anyone was saying.
As I shakily stood leaning against a wall my first
reaction was to doubt what had happened. But then
I realized what had just happened was nothing like
me. I am not emotional, I do not cry, and I'm not
easily convinced of things. As I thought about this
I knew I had to go back up to the chapel and pray.
As I entered I was a little afraid, but went in. I
found myself lying on the floor on my back with
my arms outstretched in the shape of a cross. I was
praying, but it was a very strange sensation. I was not
thinking of the words before I said them. As I
listened to what I was saying I was hearing it for
the first time. It was as if I were listening to someone
else speak. While I was doing this someone came into
chapel but I was almost not aware of the fact. After
a while I sat up and noticed it was another friend
of mine. As I looked at her praying I was so joyful
I could have burst, and I looked at her and said,
"I love you." She answered, "I love you, too," and
asked if she could read me something. She opened her
bible and started. I don't know what she read
because after the first three words I had an even more
intense encounter with Christ than before. When I
tried to speak to those who had come in I found I
could only make unintelligible sounds like a mute
trying to speak. I had so much joy and love that
I wanted to express that I couldn't do it. After a while
I did talk to those present and then left and just
walked around the house. I then related my
experience to one of the leaders (the one who gave
me the "yes" without a supporting argument) and our

chaplain. After this I returned to the chapel where I found more people praying. So I joined them.

I know I didn't get much sleep that night but the next morning I felt as rested and comforted as if I had slept all day. But the great thing was the overpowering realization that God loves *me*! Later on that day we had another talk on the third chapter of Acts. After this we prayed a little and I again encountered my God. This time I was so joyful that all I could do was laugh as I lay on the floor. I was so joyful because the Lord really cared. He knew what I needed. Boy, did he ever give it to me! He literally knocked me flat!

I found out that day that most of the people there had also had the Holy Spirit come upon them to reveal the Lord to them in a new way and to introduce a new dimension in Christian living. Well, I've been living and growing in this dimension for about a year, and believe me my whole life has been changed. The Lord has taken me by the hand and led me through many problems. But the great thing is that he is leading me to himself. I know I could never have done it alone.

Karin Sefcik

Karin Sefcik received her B.A. from Duquesne and is now doing graduate work at Michigan State University.

"Baptism in the Spirit" was a phrase Ralph Keifer seriously, yet with a bright smile on his face, brought up at an organizational meeting for our student retreat weekend at Duquesne University in February, 1967. Before a few weeks had passed I glowed like him. I, too, had been gifted richly in the "baptism in the Holy Spirit."

Having been told to remain open and expectant, waiting in prayer for God, the Yahweh of the Old Testament, the loving Father spoken of by Jesus Christ, I prayed, watched, waited, expecting the Lord to do great things for us.

After dinner Saturday night—a sloppy spaghetti supper—we discovered that the Ark and the Dove, our retreat house, had no more water. Knowing the Lord's will would be accomplished, I began to pray for enough water so that we could stay. Someone finally directed us individually to go to the chapel to pray. In the praying community there, some sang, some of us pleaded, Ralph smiled at the Lord's sense of humor. After about twenty minutes of prayer we decided to continue the evening program of short meditations. After this vigil the group dispersed. Some of us remained. By this time, explain it as you will, water had been abundantly given again. Soon Dave Mangan entered the chapel almost ecstatically. As I knelt quietly thanking the Lord, Dave lay prostrate and suddenly began to heave by the power of someone unseen. By an insight which must have been divinely inspired and by what was the beginning of my "baptism" too, I knew Dave was being moved quite visibly by the Holy Spirit. Striking changes began to take place at the Ark and the Dove.

After lunch on Sunday we sat in the conference room. I suddenly felt the peace which had pervaded within my being throughout the initial spectacular, happy outpouring of the Spirit spreading more deeply. My hands (usually cold because of poor circulation) grew moist and warm. Warmth enveloped me. I had a sense, too, that something held me back, and I wondered who would exorcise me. All day I had heard within me, "You're different, Karin, you're different." I left the room and asked someone to send in Father Healey, our chaplain for this weekend. I explained to him that I felt strange and told him I felt myself holding back. Marybeth Mutmanski and Patti Gallagher came into the room, and as Patti laid her hands on my head she exclaimed, "The Spirit of God is in you!" I began to wonder why all the fuss—I knew it was so.

The baptism in the Holy Spirit is opening my heart to more people. Often recently, especially at Mass or in chapel, my heart has begun to beat quite rapidly even as I knelt or stood quietly. The mother of God has become more special as I've come to a fuller desire to be a better woman and someday a mother. Worries plague me only briefly—until I cast my care literally upon the Lord who has sustained me well, providing time, breathing space, and energy for a gamut of activities from prayer to classes to work and school activities.

As mentioned earlier, scripture has been more opened to me since my "baptism." When I have prayed for assistance, a beautifully helpful passage has been given. The discipline of daily reading seems less a chore, more a joy now, more a kind of refreshment, challenge, or prayer.

My concern for the renewal of the Catholic

Church has grown, too. It does seem that the close attention to scripture, the desire for more participation in the liturgy (especially since in praying with Protestants I have begun to realize more fully the gift which the eucharist is) and the sheer enjoyment of praying and singing with a community can aid this renewal. My prayers include the pope, the bishop, and specific priests more often now than before.

The baptism, in short, has watered a new life for me. While I'm still quite human and forgetful, jealous, annoying, I know a richer life, a confident trust in the Lord, a closer link with the Church, a renewed concern for individuals in specific situations of need, a continually regenerated faith and confidence as I praise the Lord for his goodness, his gifts and an overflowing love. As a last comment, I must add that even laughter and joy have become richer, lighter, sprightlier. Praise the Lord!

Mary McCarthy

Mary McCarthy is a graduate student at Duquesne working for an advanced degree in history.

Before I received "baptism in the Holy Spirit" I was oftentimes a very lonely, depressed person. As one can usually see through my handwriting, my right arm is handicapped. It has been so from birth. My other physical disabilities have through my lifetime all disappeared. But before receiving the Spirit, my right arm seemed to be useless. I received

the fullness of the Spirit on April 21, 1967 at a
prayer meeting at Mr. Keifer's. Upon the Spirit's
coming I experienced bodily tremors and a sensation
of rather heavy shedding of tears. After the
Spirit's dwelling in me, I could not immediately
perceive any apparent changes in my physical or
psychological framework. But in the weeks to follow
I noticed several changes in my life. First, the
loneliness and depression vanished. Secondly, I became
more dynamically involved in the liturgy. Attendance
at daily Mass has grown to be my way of life.
Through the Mass I receive the strength I need
to witness to Christ and his teachings.

The praise of Christ has been almost constantly
in my heart and on my lips. Although I do not
possess the gift of tongues, I feel this almost
compelling urge to help, encourage, and console
others in any ways that are made manifest to me. In
short, I live my life joyously now in praise and
thanksgiving to Christ for his many blessings
given to me.

My right arm still shakes. Yet, I am now able
to use it to pick up things, such as filled glasses of
liquid, and hold them. I am even beginning to learn
to cook. Never before has this arm seemed so strong.

Today, I am happy to say that my Catholic
religion has become more dynamic for me. In my
other friends who have received the baptism, I have
perceived this same dynamic attitude. In some of
them I have witnessed the speaking in tongues,
some of which I have been able to interpret. The
messages have always been those of great solace and
joy from the Lord. Praise God!

Patricia Gallagher

*Patricia Gallagher received her B.A. from Du-
quesne and is presently in full-time apostolic
work at the Newman Center at the University
of Michigan.*

In mid-February I made a study weekend with
about thirty other students from Duquesne University
in Pittsburgh. In preparation we read *The Cross
and the Switchblade* by David Wilkerson and the
Acts of the Apostles, chapters 1-4. Although three
of our professors had already received the baptism in
the Holy Spirit a month before, none of us were
aware of this at the time. I remember after finishing
the book I knelt in my room and prayed that I
would have a deeper awareness of the Holy Spirit
and his power in my life. All references to "speaking
in tongues" and even the act of laying on hands in
the "baptism" passed me by while reading the book.
The thing which impressed me the most was how
clearly Dave Wilkerson seemed to know the will of
God. I remember wishing that I could get such
clear signs as to what the Lord wanted of me.

The next day we started discussing the chapters
in Acts. One of the professors told us that the reason
Catholics don't experience the power of the Holy
Spirit is because they don't have the faith to expect
great things from God. Just as we must constantly
reaffirm what happened to us at baptism, we need a
greater openness to the Spirit of God as we grow
and mature. He warned us that God listens and
answers our prayers and asked if we were ready for
what God would do for us. I honestly admitted I
was scared, and yet I tacked up a note on the bulletin

board which read, "I want a miracle." Some of us agreed to ask the chaplain if, as part of the closing ceremony on Sunday, we could have a renewal of confirmation vows.

In the meantime, the Lord had other plans for us. That night we had scheduled a party, but nobody seemed to be ready for light talking or dancing. I wandered up to chapel without really knowing why, but as soon as I knelt down I began to tremble. Suddenly I didn't want to leave. I remember reasoning with myself that Christ is in other people and that I should go down with them and not expect to spend my whole life in a chapel. There were three other students with me when all of a sudden I became filled with the Holy Spirit and realized that "God is real." I started laughing and crying at the same time, because not only did I know that he is real, but that he loves us. And this love that he has is almost foolish because we're so unworthy and yet he continues to freely give us his grace. I wanted to share this wonderful knowledge and joy with the others, but they seemed so detached. For a moment I thought it might just be a beautiful dream. The next thing I knew I was prostrate before the altar and filled with the peace of Christ.

I experienced what it means "to dwell in his love." In coming home to the Father who made me I felt more complete and free than ever before. I knew I was unworthy and did not have enough faith, and yet I was begging him to stay and never leave me. As much as I wanted to remain there with him I knew, just as the apostles after Pentecost, that I must share this with others. If I could experience the love and power of God in this way, anyone could. That night the Lord brought the whole group into the chapel. I found my prayers pouring forth that the others might come to know him, too. My former shyness about praying aloud was completely gone as the Holy Spirit spoke through me. The professors then laid hands on some of the students, but most of us received the "baptism in the Spirit" while kneeling before the blessed sacrament in prayer. Some of us started speaking in tongues, others received gifts of discernment, prophecy, and wisdom. But the most important gift was the fruit of love which bound the whole community together. In the Lord's Spirit we found a unity we had long tried to achieve on our own.

Coming from twelve years of public school I have always felt a real lack of religious training. This is what prompted me to join *Chi Rho,* a scripture study group on campus. I would sit at the meetings hoping to learn but always too aware of my own lack of training to say anything. About a year ago I realized that my idea of being a "good Catholic" was very weak because I didn't have a real, personal relationship with Christ. He was important to me, I prayed, even attended daily Mass, but he was not the very center of my life. By the time I made the weekend, I knew the Lord in a more personal way and found myself speaking to him in prayer frequently during the day. However, I still had problems accepting him at his word, in trusting all his commands, in believing all his promises and living my life according to them. What the world seemed to be telling me was that you can carry all this Christianity a bit too far, and that nobody really expected you to love and sacrifice yourself for others.

After all, such openness will surely lead to suffering, and you'll have only yourself to blame. Yet I felt that the Lord was saying something different and that he was calling me to put my faith in him alone.

If I had to say what effect the baptism in the Holy Spirit has had on my life, I would honestly say it has made being a Christian an exciting experience. It has given me a taste of eternal life in knowing Christ and the Father. No longer am I afraid of calling on the Holy Spirit for guidance, comfort, and power to live a Christian life. Before I received baptism in the Holy Spirit I felt as though I was living as a good Catholic. I thought I was successful, happy, and relatively free. But now I know that I had no conception of the richness of a life with Christ, that true success is achieved with him as Lord of our lives, that only he can bring us lasting joy and complete freedom, in his Spirit. I no longer feel helpless when I meet people with problems because I can lead them to God. He is faithful to his promises and steadfast in his love. His gift of the Holy Spirit is meant for all his children, but we must come to him and ask of our own free will. He is offering each of us a deeper union with him if only we answer his call. Although the baptism in the Holy Spirit does not eliminate all problems and temptations, I now know how to handle them.

Christ tells us not to be anxious because our Father knows our needs. I believe him, and when any problem or anxiety begins to trouble me I take it to the Lord and give it to him. Because of the victory of the Cross, we no longer need to fear Satan. I believe this, and ask Christ to protect and guard me with his precious blood when temptations come. He does. It is possible to be dead to sin and alive to Christ right here and now! One of the most beautiful things to experience is the real feeling of unity with fellow Christians, especially those who have received the baptism. I find myself more devoted than ever to the sacraments, especially the eucharist. The baptism in the Spirit has put life and meaning into many aspects of Catholicism which were once only tradition or habit for me. However, I know that many of my prejudices against Protestants which I never admitted I had, are beginning to melt away as the Spirit of love takes over. I find it easier to be compassionate when I ask for the mind and heart of Christ.

St. Paul's advice to the Thessalonians to pray constantly, be always joyful and give thanks whatever happens, has taken on new meaning. Through the power of the Holy Spirit one can do this. Never before did I know what it meant to praise God, but now it seems like the most fitting prayer to a Father who loves us so much that he sent his only Son that all might live. I'm not hesitant to ask the Lord for signs as to what he wants me to do. He has always been willing to speak to me but I've never been faithful or quiet enough to listen. Since this experience the Holy Spirit has taught me more about scripture than I could have learned in a whole lifetime on my own. When I read the bible now the words live because Christ lives for me. St. Paul's epistles are letters to us, too, because Jesus Christ is the same yesterday, today, and forever.

2

Growth at Notre Dame

There have been attempts to explain the pentecostal movement at Notre Dame as a return to the devotional aspects of the Church. Some say that the movement attracts people with emotional problems. Still others say it creates a false community that needs constant reinforcement. And, of course, there are those who explain the whole phenomenon in terms such as "fanatic," "cracked," "off the deep end" or "nut." But the situation is not that simple.

It would be so convenient to say that these Catholic pentecostals were underfed, high-strung, groping intellectual misfits in a wholesome atmosphere of all-American footballhood. It would be convenient, but it would also be quite untrue. There seems to be no one level of conformity in this group except a common experience.

The National Catholic Reporter

It was late January of 1967 when we heard the news that close friends of ours were about to join a charismatic prayer group and seek "baptism in the Holy Spirit." We stood huddled together on the snow-swept campus of Notre Dame, listening to Bert Ghezzi, a friend who had graduated from Duquesne University a few years earlier and who was now doing doctoral work in history at Notre Dame. To our astonishment, he told us that our good friends from Duquesne had been led in prayer to this strange step. Our reaction was immediately one of suspicion and doubt. Frankly, the situation sounded weird. Yet, we knew these people well. Binding us all was a natural trust and respect, deepened by the love of Christ. Together with our doubts and confusion, we knew very well that if these people found some good in this "laying on of hands" business, there must be something to it.

In mid-February, Ralph Keifer came out to South Bend on business and spent the weekend with us. He and a few others had by this time received the "baptism in the Holy Spirit" but the Duquesne weekend had not yet taken place. The quiet fire burning in Ralph was obvious to both of us. In a real way he was a new person, a man more centered on Christ. For two days we talked of pentecostalism and what it all could mean. Long into the nights, over many cups of coffee, we raised every intellectual, aesthetic, and psychological objection we could muster to fend off this intrusion into our religious complacency. We were curious, but quite happy to stay at a distance from the whole thing. Yet, we now had seen for ourselves a man changed by the power of the Holy Spirit. Weeks passed. One evening the phone rang. It was Ralph calling from Pittsburgh to relate the wonders of the "Duquesne weekend," urging us to read a couple of books, and to tell us that another professor and good friend of ours who also was now filled with the power of the Spirit would be out our way to visit the next weekend.

By coincidence we had already planned to hold a prayer meeting in our house the following Saturday evening, March 4, 1967. It was not unusual that a group of students and friends came together in our house that Saturday night. What we did not know is that this night would deeply change our lives. With thirty or so fellows and girls sitting around, the meeting was well under way, when our friend arrived. He did not speak until quite late in the evening, but when he did, he witnessed strongly and joyfully about the wonder of Pentecost in our own day, and how he had experienced quite literally the gifts of the Holy Spirit as recorded in the New Testament. "I do not have to believe in Pentecost," he said, "because I have seen it." Perhaps some of those present dismissed this story as curious, but others could not. The next night, March 5, nine people, including ourselves, who had decided to pursue this "baptism in the Holy Spirit" further, came together in another apartment in South Bend. After a good deal of talk, debate, and questioning, the entire group asked to be prayed with and to receive the "laying on of hands" that we might be filled with the gifts and the fruit of the Holy Spirit, that our lives might be more fully Christian.

There were, that night, no manifest charisms among the group. There was no prophecy, no speaking in tongues. There was, however, a newness in prayer, a newness that for many of us marked the beginning of a deeper faith life. We had sought in Jesus' name the fullness of the life of the Holy Spirit, and within us the change had begun. Only each one can adequately relate what happened to him or to her that night. In general, we all experienced and witnessed in each other the breakthrough of the love of Christ in our lives. With this love came the peace and joy, the faith and boldness and all these things we call the fruits of the Holy Spirit. The next day, one of the group expressed it this way to friends: "We have seen the Lord." Many were drawn to long periods of prayer, marked by the predominance of the praise of God. Some found themselves opening the bible anew with a real hunger for the word of God. Just about everyone found a new boldness in faith, a desire to witness about Jesus to friends and to strangers. Divisions, even hatreds, between brothers were healed. The love of young married couples was intensified in Christ. It was like this all throughout that first week.

On Monday, March 13, another group made up mostly of those who had received the baptism in the Holy Spirit the week before and a few newcomers went to a prayer meeting in the home of Ray and Mabel Bullard in nearby Mishawaka. Ray was president of the local South Bend chapter of the Full Gospel Businessmen's Fellowship International, an inter-faith group of laymen who share the experience of the "baptism in the Holy Spirit." We had heard of this group and thought it good to share our experience with them. If the pentecostal movement were merely a human fiction, or even a form of religiosity created out of the wills of men, it would have crumbled to dust that evening. Never would we have thought it possible for men and women, so radically different from each other in countless ways, to unite in the love of Christ. Yet, we were united by Christ. Here we were, a group of Roman Catholics, formed in the spiritual and liturgical traditions of our Church, all university trained "intellectual types." The people with whom we were meeting were mostly from an evangelical background. They spoke with a scriptural and theological fundamentalism that was very foreign to us. Furthermore, the way they spoke and prayed, the type of hymns they sang—all this was

so different that at first it was very disturbing. On the
natural level these "cultural" differences were more
than enough to keep us far apart from each other.
Yet, in spite of these personal differences, we were
enabled to come together in common faith in Jesus,
in the one experience of his Holy Spirit, to worship
our Father together. That was no human achievement.
The Holy Spirit simply cut across these cultural barriers to unite us as brothers and sisters in Christ.
Many of us received that night the gift of praising
God in strange languages.

The purpose of the gifts of the Holy Spirit is
directed toward building up the community of faith.
In the next week or two we were all preoccupied in
witnessing this faith to friends and fellow students in
our community. As each of us learned of what the
other was doing, we rejoiced to see that in each case
our testimony was not about tongues; not even
primarily about the Spirit. But wherever we went,
our talk was about Jesus Christ and the power of his
saving love to transform men and man's world.

We who had never been "pushy" apostles were
now anxious to spread the Gospel wherever we could.
When we did speak of the Holy Spirit and the here-
and-now reality of charism in the Church, we experienced from our friends the same immediate hostility
that we ourselves had felt a few weeks or months
before. Yet, again and again men from Notre Dame
and women from St. Mary's let go of their initial fear
to question and finally to seek the "baptism in the
Holy Spirit." Through a number of prayer meetings
in our homes and on the campus, more and more
students and professors, priests and nuns, lay men and
women from the South Bend area came to experience

the reality of Christ's Spirit and the same characteristics we have been noting—peace, joy, love, faith, very often accompanied by the external gifts—marked their lives. By the beginning of Holy Week and the Easter vacation, about thirty Catholics in the Notre Dame area found themselves more intent worshippers of the Father and more active witnesses to Christ through the power of the Holy Spirit.

After the Easter vacation the feeling within the community was that we needed some sort of retreat, a weekend where we could quietly come together to pray and to seek guidance from the Lord as to where we should go and what we should do. We thought that about twenty people would come and we reserved the facilities of Old College, the oldest building at Notre Dame, for that purpose on the following weekend. The Lord had other plans.

A phone call came from our friends at Michigan State University. Steve Clark and Ralph Martin maintained close contact with the Christian activities on our campus. The proximity of East Lansing to South Bend enabled us to see each other several times a year. Steve and Ralph had been interested in baptism in the Holy Spirit as long as we had. It was Steve who initially recommended Wilkerson's book *The Cross and the Switchblade* to the men in Pittsburgh. They, too, had recently received the baptism in the Holy Spirit on a visit to Pittsburgh, and word of what had happened to them was spreading on the Michigan State campus. Steve and Ralph wanted to bring a large group of students down to join our "would-be" weekend.

When the weekend (which we have come to call the "Michigan State weekend") began, we numbered about forty students, priests and faculty from Notre Dame and St. Mary's and another forty from Michigan State. Naturally we overflowed the confines of Old College and had to hold prayer meetings in large classrooms, to celebrate Mass together at the outdoor grotto of our Lady of Lourdes, and sometimes to pray and eat together while sprawled over the lawns. From Friday night till Sunday noon we lived together in a community of prayer seeking the will of God, relating our experiences to each other, discussing this new-found life from the Spirit of Christ. Throughout the weekend a large number of people from Michigan State and Notre Dame sought the "laying on of hands" so that the Holy Spirit would come to the surface in their lives. And ever and ever again did we witness prayer remarkably answered. And while we were all growing in confidence and expectation that the Lord would come, there was always the thrill and joyous surprise as Christ dealt with each individual who opened himself or herself up to him and his will. By the end of that weekend the pentecostal movement among Catholics was flourishing at Duquesne, Notre Dame, Michigan State, and offshoot groups had begun at Iowa State and Holy Cross.

The size and semi-public character of the "Michigan State weekend" brought with it a good deal of unsolicited notoriety. Report and rumor of "strange doings" spread throughout the campus. Of course the more unusual and less important elements were blown out of all proportion. "If they touched you, you would learn to speak Chinese..." "Billy Sunday or somebody was trying to make everybody Protestant..." By the end of the next week the campus publications were having a field day with the whole thing. Blared one headline, "Spiritualists Claim Gift of Tongues at Exorcism Rites." Soon the story was carried in the public press in the same more or less garbled fashion. Conclusion-jumping was rampant. Mass hypnosis! Sexual frustration! LSD!

The result of the publicity was to bring hundreds of men and women to the regular Friday night prayer meetings for the next few weeks. Some came directly to seek baptism in the Holy Spirit, and many of them did receive and rejoice in it. Many came out of sincere curiosity and open-minded interest. Others came for the fun of the non-existent but rumored "show." Reporters came from all over. Some were visibly moved. One such reporter was Mary Papa, from *The National Catholic Reporter.*

"I went to my first meeting, I think, hoping to be the first reporter in history to estimate the wingspan of the Holy Spirit. It didn't happen that way, though. Things got off the ground with an invocation of the Holy Spirit, an invitation for him to come into our midst. After that, a hymn with guitar accompaniment. And then a long period of silence—or silent prayer. I waited for something to happen. Finally, a student, who was smiling all over the place, spoke up; he thanked God and wanted to share with everyone the fact that God had helped him love a stranger in a way he never thought possible before now.

"Some random scripture readings followed. These consisted of the reader opening his bible, reading a passage aloud, then telling the group his particular insight into that passage.

"The crowd by this time had swelled to about eighty persons. Most of them were students from Notre Dame and nearby St. Mary's College, but there were also some professors, three priests, and four nuns.

"We met in a classroom almost directly beneath the Notre Dame golden dome that to many symbolizes various forms of orthodoxy. It was a stormy night and the long periods of silence were shattered by umbrellas clattering to the floor.

"As the storm progressed, the scene grew more appropriate for the strange happenings I had expected to see. But the prayers continued through a medium of cheerful conversation. A young couple held hands. A girl sipped Coke. A man offered a cigarette. And then they started singing . . . 'they'll know we are Christians by our love . . .' I felt myself being taken in."

Many, many people were "taken in." But gradually, a series of smaller, more personal prayer meetings sprang up around the campus, in the dormitories and homes of faculty members. In meetings of three or thirty people, the same wonderful work of transformation and the deepening of Christian commitment was repeated over and over again.

By the end of the semester, the thrust of the renewal had touched hundreds of Catholics across the country. Many returned home for the summer, and it was the Spirit moving us to preach the Gospel and witness to Christ. The summer months of 1967 gave rise to some new developments as we began to get reports from all over the country that our experience of the Holy Spirit was not altogether new to Catholics. Individuals had indeed received the experience, but it seemed we were the first to do so in a group.

During the summer session of 1967 about 3,000 students came as usual to the university. Composed mostly of nuns, priests, and teaching brothers, they came to do further study on advanced degrees. They came from every section of the country and were a cross-section of all the attitudes, positions and struggles that can be found in the post-Vatican II American Church. A number of us who were remaining in the city for the summer decided to set up a panel discussion on the pentecostal movement. Our purpose was not to propagate it but to explain it to these incoming students and to answer questions about it in an academic way. The story had been carried in the national Catholic press and many summer students were curious to learn just what had happened. Five of us spoke as a panel to an audience of over three hundred. Bert Ghezzi handled much of the history of the movement, and Father Edward O'Connor, C.S.C., who had observed and participated in the prayer meetings throughout the semester, discussed the movement from a theological point of view. A nun, who in the spring semester had been healed from a serious back ailment gave her testimony, as did we ourselves. There followed a good deal of questioning and healthy debate on the whole subject. We thought our obligation to the summer students duly discharged.

After the meeting about forty people expressed a desire to come to a prayer meeting. We divided them into two groups of twenty and invited one group to come Wednesday and the other on Saturday. When we reached the meeting place the first Wednesday expecting to find twenty people, we found about one hundred and fifty priests, seminarians, nuns, and lay people assembled to pray with us. It was like that twice a week for three weeks. There were upwards of 200 or more jammed into a classroom to approach the Father through Jesus. Some sought baptism in the

Holy Spirit. Others did not. But on the whole, those who came spoke of a wonderful new experience of prayer or of a deepening of prayer life that had grown cold. It was for many a discovery of what the Christian community is all about. These summer students and religious have departed from Notre Dame taking with them the spark of this renewal, this true revival, this "coming alive again" in Jesus.

About a hundred miles south of Notre Dame in the town of Elwood, Indiana, there was a growing group of charismatic Catholics. Mrs. Win Orth and a friend had come up to one of the summer meetings. They were touched by the Lord, and quickly dozens of Catholic families in Elwood received baptism in the Holy Spirit with effective exercise of the ministry gifts. Through those summer meetings the Spirit of Christ moved groups of Catholics in Dayton, Cincinnati, and Cleveland, Ohio; Kansas City and Conception, Missouri; Portland, Oregon; and Denver, Colorado. From one end of the land to the other on campuses, among families, among laity and clergy, the mystery of the risen Christ became more wonderfully real and powerfully present in the lives of hundreds of Catholics.

In the fall of 1967, Steve Clark and Ralph Martin moved on from Michigan State and the charismatic community in Lansing to the University of Michigan in Ann Arbor. There they were joined by Gerry Rauch and Jim Cavnar, who had been among the first at Notre Dame to experience baptism in the Holy Spirit. The four are now based at Michigan working at the campus Newman Center to preach the word and to build up the body of Christ.

More recently we met three Benedictine monks at

a Full Gospel Business Men's banquet in Zion, Illinois. After the meeting we prayed together for the fullness of the life of the Spirit in them and in their monastery. Today in a community of thirty or forty priests and brothers, about twenty participate in spontaneous prayer meetings and fifteen or so including the abbott and other religious superiors have received baptism in the Holy Spirit, praising God in tongues.

Our suspicion that this experience of renewal, now widespread, was not new to American Catholics was confirmed as we heard of, or received letters from, individuals and groups of Catholics around the land. From Florida, California, Texas, Wisconsin, Massachusetts, we learn of the quiet work of the Holy Spirit over the years.

Looking back now at the end of the second year of the Catholic pentecostal movement, from summer 1967 to summer 1968, we can see many more signs pointing to a continual and rapid growth of this renewal. Our mailing list is hopelessly out of date. We receive notices of Catholic pentecostal days of renewal organized by people we have never heard of.

"Did you hear about the group of thirty or so in Akron? . . No, but there are several groups in Washington, about ninety there have received baptism in the Holy Spirit . . . State of Washington? . . No, D.C.; but there's a group in the state too . . . What's the address of a prayer group in New York City? . . It was in Mount Vernon but now it's in Rockaway, but if that's too far there's another one just across the bridge in Jersey." It is like this day after day as word is confirmed from all over the United States and

Canada that the Holy Spirit is being poured out on hundreds of people with little or no human connection or organized effort. It is a conservative estimate that as this book goes to press there are at least 5,000 Catholic pentecostals in the United States and several hundred in Canada.

With considerable regularity there are week-long or weekend conferences of students and faculty from the various Catholic and state universities. Such a meeting was held in Boulder, and another in Vancouver. Typical was one held at Notre Dame in September of 1967. To a week of praying, sharing, and living together in Christ came undergrads and coeds from Michigan State, the University of Michigan, Duquesne, Iowa State and Notre Dame, and St. Mary's as well as lay men and women from throughout the mid-west. From the freewheeling prayer sessions of this conference came the plans, the hope, and the faith for a year of campus apostolate that has been felt across the land.

In contrast to such youthful zip, are the more sedate activities of a group of middle-aged Catholic couples in and around Boca Raton, Florida. Meeting in the home of Dr. Susan Anthony, Associate Professor of Theology at Marymount College, this group began to meet early in 1968. These people are a good example that pentecostalism is not just a young people's movement. The tone may be more reserved, the hymns perhaps more traditional, because such elements develop spontaneously from the group itself. But the experience of the Holy Spirit is the same, the same transformation, the same ministry gifts. Which all goes to prove that the Holy Spirit can work effectively in the strangest places, even under the south Florida palm trees.

One of the most notable events of the year was the Memorial Day Weekend Conference on Charismatic Renewal conducted under the aegis of Father James Short, S.M., at the Bergamo Retreat Center in Dayton, Ohio. This conference brought together such well-known scholars as Barnabas Ahern, Josephine Ford, Kilian McDonnell and Edward O'Connor for a discussion of the pros and cons of pentecostalism within Catholicism. Not merely an exercise in academe, the conference carried on in an atmosphere of prayer and the praise of God. In its June 14, 1968 issue, *Time* reported on the conference under the headline, "Charisma on the Rise":

"This month an ecumenical assembly of 120 churchmen met at Roman Catholic Dayton University in Ohio to discuss the movement . . . Surprisingly, even some Roman Catholic participants at the Dayton conference were cautiously optimistic about the prospect of incorporating glossalalia and healing into the spirituality of their church. Biblical scholar Barnabas Mary Ahern, a *peritus* (expert) at the Second Vatican Council, argued that glossalalia should be 'running at the very heart of the Church' since 'the life of the Church is the life of the Spirit.'"

Whether in such impressive assemblies or in lunch hour prayer breaks of a few students, the charismatic movement continues to spread. But for those of us at Notre Dame, the outstanding event of 1968 was the conference on renewal in the Holy Spirit in March. Because it was so deeply meaningful to all of us, yet so typical, we describe it in detail.

"Put on then, as God's chosen ones, holy and beloved, compassion, kindness, lowliness, meekness, and patience, forbearing one another and, if one has a complaint against another, forgiving each other; as the Lord has forgiven you, so you also must forgive. And above all these put on love, which binds everything together in perfect harmony. And let the peace of Christ rule in your hearts, to which indeed you were called in one body. And be thankful. Let the word of Christ dwell in you richly, as you teach and admonish one another in all wisdom, and as you sing psalms and hymns and spiritual songs with thankfulness in your hearts to God. And whatever you do, in word or deed, do everything in the name of the Lord Jesus, giving thanks to God the Father through him" (Col. 3, 12-17).

With this exhortation of St. Paul to guide us, the weekend conference on renewal in the Holy Spirit began on the campus. As the first meeting began on Friday night, approximately one hundred Christians, aglow with the Spirit, began to meet each other in prayer and in love. From Texas, Florida, Pennsylvania, Massachusetts, New York, Ohio, Michigan, Illinois, Indiana, and Ontario, we gathered to "teach and admonish one another in all wisdom," to "sing psalms and hymns" and to give praise to the name of the Lord Jesus.

The opening meeting was characterized by prayers of praise, as we shared the good news of what the Spirit had been doing in the different communities represented. Through the gifts of prophecy and wisdom, the group found directions from the Lord toward greater awareness and involvement in the grave and pressing human concerns of war, race relations, and poverty. Again and again we were pointed toward the realization that our responsibility is as great as the power of the Spirit who moves us. As a concrete tangible sign of our willingness to begin at least to follow these promptings of the Spirit, Jim Byrne, a Notre Dame senior, was inspired to suggest that the money which had been collected for Saturday's dinner should be turned over instead to Father William Manseau of Boston for his work with the poor in the inner city. It was, and prayer and songs of praise continued into the night. The rich harmony of "singing in tongues" arose spontaneously several times as the joy of meeting all these new brothers and sisters in Christ sought expression. The evening closed as it had begun, with Jim Cavnar of Ann Arbor leading us with his guitar in a rousing version of Psalm 150. A tambourine rang out as well. "Let everything that has breath, praise the Lord!"

Saturday morning, the sun across the lake and the chirping song birds met us at the outdoor grotto of Our Lady as we opened the day with prayer. It was obvious that the ranks swelled during the night to about two hundred. Father Edward O'Connor of Notre Dame led us in Lauds, the morning hour of the Divine Office. After coffee, donuts and hello's we gathered in the Administration Building, under the golden dome, for the morning meeting. Prior to this session, Ralph Martin of Ann Arbor, who was to give the main talk, was prayed with that the Spirit would anoint him and fill him with the gift of preaching. In powerful and penetrating words, we heard the Lordship of Jesus proclaimed. Jesus is Lord of all creation; of men, of work, of fun, of study, of plants, of animals, of all that is lofty and all that is lowly. He is Lord of rich and poor, of hippies and squares, of those who earn doctorates, of those who wash dishes. In him all things hold together. Unity, love, universal Lordship—we must learn them well. A "listening time" formed a response to the word which the Lord had given us. After lunch the afternoon was arranged into a series of workshops where each participant could get down to the nitty gritty of life in the Spirit, learning ways of witnessing to Christ, the principles of prayer life, the exercise of the gifts of the Spirit, the scriptural background to the baptism in the Holy Spirit, the integration of charismatic life and liturgical celebration.

A concelebrated eucharist climaxed the events of the day. Father Manseau gave the homily, and it reinforced our direction toward involvement in the concerns of society. We must share with all of God's children the gifts, the power and love which we have received. Before the offertory of the Mass, Tom Bettler, a Notre Dame senior, made his profession of faith and was officially received into the Catholic Church and received his first communion. All the more reason to celebrate!

After a chicken dinner as we relaxed and prepared for the evening session, prayer, song and reflections on our life in Christ formed the evening meeting. The many sanctions for the charismatic Christian to be found in the documents of Vatican II were noted by Father O'Connor who set the tone of the reflections. We were sleepy. The meeting was a brief one, but the presence of God never waned. Before the meeting ended the Lord spoke to us through tongues and interpretation. "I reach out my hand to you. You need only take it and I will lead you." Prayer rooms were opened after the meeting for instruction and counseling by designated leaders. The Spirit of the Lord met each one who asked in faith, with his peace and his power.

Sunday morning we met in the beautiful and impressive chapel of Moreau Seminary on the lake at Notre Dame. The richness of the liturgy, the full unity of the eucharist drew us together, and in the homily the Lord gave us a sign of his leadership and presence in our weekend. Father Walter Hanss of Rochester, New York, had been asked to give the homily at the closing eucharist. On Saturday night as he tried to prepare for his talk one sentence kept repeating in his mind. He wrote it down and used it as the theme for his outline. His task done, he rejoined the end of the prayer meeting just as Dave Mangan of Pittsburgh was giving the interpretation to a message in tongues. Joyfully, but not really with surprise, we heard Father Hanss tell us in his closing homily that the words which the Lord had given him to preach were the same words which he heard given in interpretation as he rejoined the prayer meeting the night before. "I reach out my hand to you. You need only take it and I will lead you." Wherever our paths led from this weekend, to witness and work for Jesus, it was not alone. The walk is with Jesus. He leads. On this note of celebration the conference concluded.

It is most important to note that the outpouring of the Holy Spirit in these days has occured to Catholics *within* the Catholic Church. The pentecostal movement has not separated or excluded Catholics from their Church. Rather it has renewed their love of the Church and has built up a lively faith in the Catholic community.

While the movement is authentically Catholic, it

has brought about a new dimension in the ecumenical relations among Christians. In recent months the Holy Spirit has brought us into fellowship not only with Christians from Pentecostal Churches, but also with charismatic Christians within the historical Protestant Churches. Furthermore, we have met with many Evangelical Christians who do not accept pentecostalism but with whom we share the saving love of Jesus.

For centuries brick walls of fear and distrust have been built between Christians of different denominations. To heal the scandal, the Churches in the last fifty years have entered ecumenical dialogue which at times has had wonderful results and at other times hit a dead end of failure and frustration. Today, by the work of the Spirit among us, some of those old bricks have been knocked loose, and on a person-to-person level we are encountering each other for the first time in an experience of the love of Jesus. We now see Catholics and Evangelicals sitting down together around the Word, in the common experience of salvation to praise our Father with one voice in unity and in love. Our unity is by no means complete, we have still many differences of doctrine and practice, but the unity we share in faith in Jesus and in the praise of the Father and in the life of the Holy Spirit is genuine. Thus, what we have been unable to accomplish by ourselves all these years, has been worked among us by the Holy Spirit.

The experience of the baptism in the Holy Spirit is so rich and varied—for the Lord is pouring out his Spirit on the Church, is baptizing unique individuals, changing and fulfilling the lives of persons—that it is impossible in this book to sufficiently summarize this beautiful sharing in the life of Christ. Only the men and women touched by the Spirit of God can adequately share (and then often with a feeling of inadequacy) the depth of Jesus' love for them. For this reason we present a series of typical testimonies of Christians who have received baptism in the Holy Spirit during the growth of the pentecostal movement at Notre Dame.

BEARING WITNESS

James Cavnar

James Cavnar graduated magna cum laude from Notre Dame in 1967 with a B.A. in theology. He is now employed in apostolic work at the Newman Center in Ann Arbor.

"He shall wipe every tear from their eye..."

"I no longer believe in Pentecost, I've seen it." I, too, can now say this when friends want to know what's happened. Because I've been seeing all the things that happened at Pentecost—men speaking in new tongues, prophecy, healing, the Gospel preached with conviction and power, and lives deeply changed by God. I've not only seen Pentecost in others, but I've seen it in myself.

I grew up in a good Catholic family, attending Catholic schools through grade school and high school. It was not unusual for me to be involved in a number of Christian organizations throughout high school, even to hold leadership positions in them. I graduated at the top of my class in high school and went on to college at Notre Dame, not only because it was a good university but because it was Catholic. Through my first year at Notre Dame I continued to be active in Christian organizations, convinced that Christianity was important. But like many

58

university students I soon found my Christianity disturbing. I began to notice that there was little that I did that was uniquely Christian. Except for Sunday Mass my actions could have been done (and were being done) by a good humanist. I began to find Christianity more and more not making a difference in the way I lived from day to day. "What's the difference between a Christian and a humanist?" I asked, and more often than not I was told, "Nothing." And so I dropped out of any Christian organizations—my ideals and goals could as well be achieved without the tag "Christian." By sophomore year I began to find my thought and my deepest feelings most accurately articulated not by the bible or the Church but by writers and philosophers. They were the ones who recognized, as I did, that life was without ultimate meaning, that it was "absurd," as absurd as a Christianity that could offer the man who lives from day to day nothing beyond what any intelligent, humanly sensitive person could see. I continued going to Church on Sunday, but I lived the life of an agnostic— Christianity made no difference to what I did, said, hoped. I knew it was like that. And I knew that if something did not happen soon, I would abandon even my nominal Christian exterior. I also knew that I was near the end. To discover that life is without meaning is a liberating experience and brings a happy freedom—but it also brings, eventually, an inescapable and oppressive despair, a despair that is unhappy, that offers no reason to live, that steals the desire to live. Despair was stealing life from me.

It was at the end of my sophomore year that things

changed. Through the efforts of a friend I ended
up on a Cursillo (a type of retreat) in South Bend.
During the three days of the Cursillo I heard laymen
from South Bend talk about the Christian life,
and I discussed it in groups of men. And I suddenly
saw, in a perfectly clear, lucid, and life-shattering
way what the difference was that Christianity made:
the difference was Christ. To be a Christian meant
having a personal relationship with another person
—Christ himself; and it meant living in union
with other Christians with Christ; it meant
introducing others to Christ. What Christianity
offered that no other philosophy could, was not an
ideal, an idea, an ethic, or a doctrine, but the *living*
Jesus of Nazareth.

My life was radically changed overnight. Despair
vanished before the incredible joy and purposefulness
of knowing Christ. I began praying daily, reading
scripture, and taking every opportunity to share
Christ with others. And I began to see that this
was the most important thing in the world, all else
was nothing by comparison. And I began to devote
the great majority of my time to growing in
Christianity and in working to bring others to Christ
at Notre Dame. After much prayer, I changed my
major from physics to theology to better prepare
myself for what I hoped would be a life in the
Christian apostolate.

But despite this, when I came in contact with
the baptism in the Holy Spirit in March of my senior
year, I wanted nothing to do with it. For in the
two months prior to my baptism in the Holy Spirit
I had been experiencing what I can only describe

as the worst depression of my life. Suddenly,
inexplicably, I had found myself under a constant
burden, unable to be cheerful or charitable, finding
my regular daily prayer nearly impossible, scripture
hard to look at, my apostolic work a terrible burden.
With the greatest of difficulty I continued my
prayer and witnessing, but try as I might, nothing
I could do seemed to be able to free me from this
depression. And it grew worse. I found myself
constantly fighting off overwhelming feelings of
resentment when people would ask me to do even
the smallest thing for them, even when they so much
as talked with me. I remember that the only prayer
I could pray was "Lord, I don't understand why
you're doing this to me. I'm willing to trust you
know what you're doing, but help me soon!" And, as
I told my spiritual director, "I've never in my life
felt so utterly helpless. In the face of this depression
I am helpless." It was this feeling of helplessness
that was the hardest to bear because it slowly
eroded hope. I remember praying once and feeling
deep inside, so deep that I couldn't fathom it, an
obstacle to God. Like a stone deep in my heart,
sitting there as a heavy weight too deep for me to
reach it and move it. All I could pray was "Lord, I
trust you. Help me soon."

When a friend told me that a group of students
from Duquesne University had experienced the
baptism in the Spirit, I wanted nothing to do with it.
Waves of resentment had begun to harden my heart
to anything Christian, including this. And so when
I was told that a professor from Duquesne was coming
to a prayer meeting and would be telling us what
had happened, I absolutely didn't want to go. But

another friend made me promise to come. Out of stubbornness I did.

I sat in stony silence during the prayer meeting, unwilling and unable to speak as we listened to him tell of students speaking in tongues, prophesying, and being the instruments of remarkable conversions. The story he told was truly amazing. All I could think, though, was: "If you all are interested in this stuff, okay, I won't get in the way. But I want nothing to do with it." I knew it was a bad attitude to take; I was convinced that he spoke the truth and that the experiences described were probably authentic—but hardness and resentment were the passion of my heart and no reasoning could change the fact that I felt as I did.

But at the end of the prayer meeting, something happened. The professor began to pray, and I was struck by the power and conviction of his prayer. I thought: "Here is a man who speaks with authority, who really knows what he is talking about. This must have been the kind of authority people saw in Christ." And as he began to pray, I decided to make a real effort to pray with him. And so I struggled to repeat in my mind each word he said. He prayed for two things: first, that we would all be free from any power of Satan, and second, that we would be filled with the Spirit. It couldn't have taken more than two minutes.

I woke up the next morning like a different person. The depression of two months was entirely gone and I felt naturally cheerful and bouyant, eager to be with others, desirous of praying and reading the bible, filled with a spirit of charity. I was aware that what had happened to me was clearly

not my own doing. I had been utterly helpless before
to break the deadlock on my Christian life. Now
it had happened to me and was clearly the work of
God alone, not me. And later that night the Lord
showed me what he had done. For that night nine
of us gathered with the Duquesne professor for
prayer, and we asked him to lay hands on us and
pray for the baptism in the Spirit. I was the last to
ask, but now, freed from oppression, I was eager to.

And so he went around to us one by one—I was
last. He first commanded in the name of Jesus that
Satan depart from us, free us from his temptations,
doubts, and obstacles, and leave us free to respond
fully to God. And then he laid on hands and
prayed for us to be filled with the Holy Spirit. It
was quiet—silent except for his voice. As each one was
prayed over, he seemed to sink into silent and deep
prayer. There were no tongues that first night, no
immediate exuberance.

When he came to me I really didn't look for
any outward manifestation. I knew that the baptism
in the Spirit was received in faith by asking the Father
for the outpouring of the Spirit promised by his
Son. I felt that the most important thing was to
ask in faith, with confidence in God and full of
expectation that because I had asked in faith, he
would truly fulfill his promises and pour out his
Spirit in a powerful way. And I really felt confidence
that the Spirit would be given.

He stood before me for a moment, and then, in
Christ's name, cast out Satan. As soon as he said
the words I knew that a demon had left. I felt myself
physically shaken and smelled clearly and distinctly
the smell of burning sulphur, a smell I know well

from chemistry lab. And immediately I knew what had
happened. God was allowing me a sign that what had
been oppressing me for two months and before
which I had felt helpless was the power of Satan.
And I had been helpless before him, for only God
had the power to overcome him. And the Lord
showed me in this sign that he had overcome him and
that it had been God's power that had broken the
devil's oppression the night before, and that cast
him out entirely now. Immediately I felt a tremendous
sense of thanksgiving to God for doing this for me,
for freeing me from the deadening oppression of evil
which I had borne like a great weight for so long.
I felt a great happiness that he had done this for
me and that he had given me this sign so I would
know beyond doubt what he had done.

    Hands were then laid on me, and though I
didn't receive tongues that first night so many things
began happening that week that I was reassured
beyond doubt of the power of the Holy Spirit. I
suddenly found myself strongly drawn to the
scriptures. They seemed transparent to me. Prayer
became a real joy—the sense of the presence and love
of God was so strong that I can remember sitting in
the chapel for a half hour just laughing out of joy
over the love of God. As I began talking with others,
a strange thing happened: I began to feel that I
knew exactly what to say to them and what they
needed to hear, even guys that I hardly knew. I
found that the Holy Spirit gave me a real boldness
to say it and it had a marked effect. I found out
that the same things were happening to the other
people who had been prayed over with me. After
two months of experiencing complete helplessness

to overcome depression, I was experiencing a joy and power that I knew wasn't from me—it could have come only from the Holy Spirit.

Since that week in March, many things have happened. The baptism in the Spirit and receiving tongues now seem but a beginning compared to the great things that God has done since. For growth in the life of Christ means receiving grace upon grace as the love of God penetrates deeper and deeper. And because of what was begun in the baptism in the Spirit, I have now begun to see more and more a vision of what life in the Spirit is like. It is truly a life of miracles, of waiting on God for his guidance and teaching, of relying on the power of the Spirit to radically change the lives of men, and of being filled over and over with the creative, life-giving love of the Spirit of God. "What no eye has seen, nor ear heard, nor the heart of man conceived, what God has prepared for those who love him, God has revealed to us through the Spirit" (1 Cor. 2, 9-10).

Thomas Noe

Tom Noe is a senior at Notre Dame in 1969. He is editor of the Leprechaun, *a student literary publication, and is religion commissioner of Farley Hall, an undergraduate residence.*

I was a sophomore at the University of Notre Dame when everything started happening there in the spring of 1967. Up until that time, my connection with the Holy Spirit was only through my imperfect understanding of his role in baptism and confirmation, both of which I had passed over without encountering the knowledge of the fullness of freedom that comes with realization of the Holy Spirit's power. I was one who had still not asked the Father for the guidance of the Spirit.

The first faint manifestations of the Spirit's intentions for me began before I had even heard of the pentecostal experience as applied to Catholics, and indeed when I still regarded pentecostal groups as just a bit off their collective rockers with unchecked emotionalism and irrational fundamentalism.

During Easter vacation in 1967 I had stayed at school to do a term paper assigned for my theology class. We had discussed the topic of mystical language in class, and my interest in this subject (I planned to major in English philology) led me to the library for further research. I happened to come across several references to speaking in tongues, and soon I had (coincidentally?) chosen this as the topic of my term paper. Hindsight convinces me that the Holy Spirit was preparing me for his fuller revelation in a few weeks. I started researching merrily along, even encountering references to the emergence of this particular gift in connection with the growing pentecostal movement in the more traditional Protestant Churches. I didn't find, nor did I expect to find, references to any such movement in the Catholic Church.

Then, still during Easter break, a group of students who had gone up to Michigan State University for Easter services returned to Notre Dame. The Wednesday after Easter found me in room 244 Farley Hall, discussing nothing in particular with three students who had just returned. John Kirby asked me the name of the paper that was taking up my Easter vacation, and when I calmly replied that it was on tongue-speaking, his jaw dropped down amid his toes. He turned to Jim Cavnar and Jerry Rauch to tell them the subject. They both looked at John, then looked at each other, and finally turned to me. "Tom," said Jim, grinning, "do you know what's been going on around here?" Their strange reaction hinted that the question demanded a curious "no" for an answer. I curiously "no'ed."

Then the research from my paper really paid off, for I was told that several people in the hall actually spoke in tongues, and that even more had received baptism in the Holy Spirit. I took it all matter-of-factly and nonplussedly asked when the next prayer meeting was.

That night I found myself at Kevin's house for a prayer meeting. I asked for the laying on of hands. I was so confident that the Spirit would be true to his word that I prayed without using any if's. I prayed in will's and shall's and in every other kind of declarative statement. My readings (all non-scriptural, I must confess) had convinced me that the power of the Holy Spirit was real and relevant for men today.

When hands were laid upon me, immediately it felt as if my whole chest were trying to rise into my head. My lips started trembling, and my brain started turning flips. Then I started grinning; I couldn't help it. He had faithfully answered his promise, and I knew that the Spirit was now going to stay with me, to help me preach the good news of Christ

and to worship God in a fuller way than I could have
done otherwise.

I went back to my dormitory room and stayed
up until 3 A.M. reading the books of Psalms and
Acts. I couldn't put the bible down. I wanted to read
more and more, to read both of the glory and power
of Yahweh and the glory and power of the apostles
transformed through the Spirit.

The biggest problem I had after baptism in the
Spirit was finding enough outlets for my apparently
limitless ability to pray to or praise God for any
reason, at any time of the day. I was constantly
reading the bible, treking down to chapel, and when
I wasn't talking I was humming hymns to myself.
If this had happened when school was on, I probably
would have flunked out, but it would have been
great doing it.

I didn't receive the one gift I was researching
in my term paper at the prayer meeting, but the
absence of tongues didn't worry me. I had felt too
much of the overwhelming presence of God to be
concerned that I still had to praise and thank him
in English. It was after school began again, about
two and one-half weeks later, that I was sitting
waiting for theology class to start and using the time
to pray the rosary (a practice I've taken up since
baptism in the Spirit). There were several others
in the room also waiting, and so I prayed silently,
moving my lips to the prayers. I was very quiet and
meditative throughout, and the only out of the
ordinary thing that happened was that after I finished
the last prayer, my lips decided to keep moving, and
rearranged themselves into a confusion of p's, k's
and l's. I was just about to start speaking out loud in

tongues when I remembered that there were ignorant
bystanders around who might be quite upset to
witness such an outburst. So I thought, "Stop!"
and notwithstanding the immense sense of joy and
happiness of closeness to God that made me want to
raise my arms in the air and shout out the glory
of God, I made it through the class. One thing,
though. I was naturally grinning broadly, and the
teacher was quite disturbed to have one of his
students ignore his lecture and grin steadily at him
for an entire class period. Later that day I first used
my tongue in prayer and it has since become a
valuable part of my entire prayer experience.

The baptism in the Spirit and the things that have
come out of it have changed my life in one particular
area where I was doubtful of any possibility of
change. The main difficulty I was under previous
to the "baptism" was an unwillingness to admit my
total reliance on God as creator, redeemer, and
sustainer. I couldn't surrender my will totally to the
will of Christ. I had attended a study weekend at
Notre Dame, a shortened form of the Cursillo, and
had come to acknowledge that Christ is indeed the
focal point of every man's existence. But I had
simply *acknowledged* this—I still had not fully
implemented this in my life, in my relationships with
others. I still had an overconfidence in myself, in my
own capacities and abilities, in the belief that I
could run my own life by myself and still come out
ahead in the end. I have always been self-reliant
and self-sufficient, making decisions entirely on my
own, regarding the advice of others as more of a
reflection of their own opinions than as anything that
should influence my own beliefs. This was the part

of me that most needed change—and change it did.

The Spirit has deepened every aspect of my religious experience. I have found a new level of meaning in all the sacraments, especially in confession and the eucharist. I have come to a greater realization of the eucharist as sacrifice, and I have returned to frequent confession where before I was doubtful of its value as a corrective agent. I have found a deep devotion to Mary, and I can now praise God—something I had never been able to do before. I've developed a capacity to love people in a way impossible for me before. I glorify God in a freedom that comes only from the Spirit, and my faith has developed to a level I never thought attainable except by saints. My temper has disappeared, and I am consistently happier than I have ever been before.

I can acknowledge my dependence on God in a way that coaxes me to go out and tell others of the redemption effected by Christ. I count this as the most valuable gift I have received from the Holy Spirit—this new boldness in speaking out about Christ. And with the continuing help of his Spirit, I am sure that miracles are no longer impossible— for my own change was certainly a personal miracle. What might be a less imposing miracle is the fact that I got an A on my term paper.

Anne Johnson

Anne Johnson graduated from St. Mary's College in 1968 as a Christian Culture major. She is presently employed by the Catholic Social Services of Detroit.

For the past two years many beautiful things have happened to me. I have discovered God. It is as simple as that. I have been raised a Catholic and have been educated in Catholic schools all my student life. I thought I loved God and I never really thought much about his love for me; that was taken for granted. I heard the same things the rest of my classmates heard. Nothing extraordinary went into my religious instruction. My faith was never questioned because I didn't care enough about it to question. It was there, something to put up with, to learn to exist with because it was the only thing to do. I was what people so tritely call, a "Sunday Catholic." I attended Mass on Sunday and on holy days of obligation because my family went and because it was what every good Catholic did. So I felt I had all the qualifications of being a good Catholic.

It wasn't until my sophomore year at St. Mary's College that things began to change. Someone decided that it was time for me to discover Christ. That someone was in reality two people, my brother John and a new theology teacher at the college, Kevin Ranaghan. My brother asked me to make a weekend with a group of girls at the college I attended. He told me it was not a retreat but an opportunity for me to learn about Christ. Well, I thought I knew about Christ, having gone through the Baltimore Catechism cover to cover in addition to thirteen years of Catholic instruction. I was very wrong. This weekend in late September of 1965 opened my eyes wide to Christ. I experienced love of Christ for the first time in myself. I was beginning to see what was meant by living Christianity. It was slow, because of all the skepticism and doubt I had unknowingly built up over the years, but it was a beginning. Kevin brought Christ alive in the classroom. Learning about Christ-became real and exciting and something. What I was beginning to realize was to be very important in my life as a Christian: If I was to love God, I first had to know about him.

Things really started to happen. I was learning about God, and I was beginning to see what was meant by living a Christian life. We had a community of students from both St. Mary's and Notre Dame. We met every Monday and Friday for Mass and usually one other night during the week. As we worshipped together and at our gatherings afterward, we grew closer as a community. Most of us became very close to one another, and I was beginning to realize that these people were becoming the most important people in my life. Kevin became the one person I was closest to. I found myself opening up to him and talking to him as I had never done with anyone before. He pulled me through all my academic, social and spiritual crises that year. I began to learn the importance of community and the meaning of sharing your love of Christ with those you loved. Then summer came and I was miserable. The community had dispersed throughout the country, and except for letters I felt isolated and alone. My brother talked to me and helped me, gave me advice and comfort, but he was only one person, and he was trying to make up for thirty. It just couldn't be done. I missed these

people and I believed once I returned to school
I'd be fine again.

Kevin returned to St. Mary's in the fall, and with
him came his beautiful wife of less than one month,
Dorothy. I had signed up for his theology course
and was very excited. I spent a lot of time with
them that first semester, and they grew to be my
closest and most trusted friends. I found myself
talking about them so much during my Christmas
vacation that I know my family was beginning to
wonder what had happened to me. I could explain
to no one how I felt about those people. They
were two beautiful people who loved God more
than anything or anyone. They overflowed with
love of God. We were involved with the community
on both campuses.

The Mass and the gatherings continued much the
same way as they had during the previous year, with
a few new faces now and then. I was satisfied. I
believed I was leading the best possible Christian
life I could at that moment. The Ranaghans and
I spent much time talking about the Christian
community at St. Mary's, for we all believed that
many of the students at the college had not really
discovered Christ; he was not important to them.
We worked with one of the chaplains at the college
on the liturgy, but the response from students was
virtually nothing. Kevin asked if we could meet
with several other girls every morning to pray for
guidance in our lives. We did. Eventually, we decided
to have a prayer meeting at Kevin and Dorothy's
home. It was to be just an ordinary prayer meeting
with students from both campuses.

About this time I remember hearing about

some people in Pittsburgh, and I also remember thinking they were pretty strange people. Dorothy is from Pittsburgh and had gone to Duquesne University. Kevin had some former friends there too. They were the people they were telling me about. I first heard about baptism in the Holy Spirit from Kevin. He tried to explain it to me one day but didn't understand it yet himself, thought it was weird, and thought our sacraments of baptism and confirmation would serve just as well. I agreed, knowing less about it than he did. But already I was afraid. I was afraid of anything that would hurt my little community or that would disrupt my beliefs in Christianity.

A few days before our prayer meeting, I saw Kevin between classes. He told me one of the men from Pittsburgh was coming to Notre Dame that weekend and would be at the prayer meeting that coming Saturday night. I had always wanted to meet this person because he was very important to Dorothy, and I had had the feeling that he had been to Dorothy what Kevin was to me. I was rather excited about meeting him and couldn't understand why Kevin and Dorothy were so hesitant about his arrival.

But when he spoke at the prayer meeting I knew why they felt the way they did. He was involved with this "baptism" stuff I had been hearing about. It wasn't until he spoke that I realized there was something different about him. I recall being amazed at the way he spoke and was frightened of the confidence with which he spoke. It was his confidence that made him appear so different. When he prayed it seemed as if he were demanding

God to answer his prayers. Then he spoke of
Pentecost. He said he no longer believed in Pentecost
on faith because he had witnessed it. He told us
of the happenings in Pittsburgh that had changed
the lives of many college students there. I remember
my reaction that night: virtually nothing! I was
happy to be there with my friends; I was happy
to be praying with them. It wasn't until the beginning
of the next week that I began to notice a change
within my community. I first became aware of the
change in Kevin one morning during morning
prayer. His prayer took on the same kind of
confidence I had noticed in his friend. He no longer
asked God for help, it was now more of a sure
confidence that he would receive the help because he
had demanded it in faith. This really scared me
because it was someone I knew who was praying this
way. Afterward when I tried to ask him how he
was and why he was changed, I found myself closed
and very bitter to all he was trying to say. Kevin,
knowing me as he did, told me not to worry, that God
would open my heart to his Spirit.

I didn't like the idea at all. I grew more bitter as
the week went on. Then I soon discovered that
the baptism in the Spirit was happening to many
of my friends at Notre Dame. Several of my closest
friends really threw me. They were still the beautiful
people I knew, yet they had changed. They didn't
seem the least upset because I disapproved of how
they were acting. What they cared about was
God. What they lived for now was a deeper sense
of spiritual awareness of the love, power, and
influence that the Holy Spirit was having in their lives.
They still loved, they still joked and laughed,

they were the same and yet they were changed. They told me not to worry, that my fear and skepticism would be taken away because God loved me and his Spirit would manifest himself in me. They were confident of this because they had prayed for this with faith and trust in the Holy Spirit. I think if the Holy Father in Rome had told me not to worry and not to be skeptical it wouldn't have made the slightest bit of difference. I was afraid and worried that my best friends had become religious fanatics and would soon crack. With all my questions, oppositions, and open bitterness they would only smile and say not to worry. It was the smile that would always get me because it was genuine and I knew that they meant it. There was no doubt about it in my mind. These people had changed. I did not want to change, therefore, I knew I would have to stay away from them.

It didn't work though, especially with Kevin whom I saw daily at school. My favorite phrase to him was "keep your hands to yourself," meaning that at no time did I ever have the intention of being prayed over. It was said jokingly—and we always laughed—but he knew I meant it. I was afraid God might want this, and I knew that if I was prayed over, perhaps he would take over. I was not convinced that I should let God take over. Being the proud female I am, I wanted to solve my problems myself without any outside help. Yet, at the same time I was convinced that I trusted in God.

With all their pestering I knew that sooner or later I would have to go to one of their prayer meetings. When the day arrived, I could think of nothing else. My mind was whirling with excuses to try and get out of going. It was useless, I was stuck; there was no doubt about it. I sat in my chair during the first part of that meeting with a hate I never knew I had. I hated them, I hated God, and I hated myself for coming. I wanted to leave but I couldn't get up the courage I needed to leave them. I loved them. With all their crazy ideas about God and the Holy Spirit, I loved *them.*

Then something happened. One of the boys that had not been prayed with yet read a passage from scripture. It was from John 14, 18-31, and as he read that passage something came over me. I knew I'd never be able to explain it, but I know it was the beginning—my beginning. Verse 18 of chapter 14 says: "I will not leave you orphans; I will come to you." That had always been my favorite passage from scripture; whenever I read the bible I always turned there first. Whenever I was depressed or confused I always read that passage; it seemed to help each time. Each time I would receive a new insight; God would give me something more from reading it. And now I was receiving a new message. As the boy read the passage, I felt God was opening my heart wide to his goodness, his love, and his Spirit was visibly present to me in these people in the room with me. In that same chapter, Christ continues to speak and he says: "These things I have spoken to you while I am still with you. But the Counselor, the Holy Spirit, whom the Father will send in my name, he will teach you all things, and bring to your remembrance all that I have said to you." Further he states: "Let not your hearts be troubled, neither let them be afraid."

He read on, and as he did, I realized that that
passage was read for a purpose. It had not been
planned by anyone there except the Holy Spirit
whose power permitted it to be read. I realize this
probably makes no sense; I know I probably sound
crazy when I say I know that passage was read
for me. I know God wanted me to be open to his
Spirit that he told us he would send to us. It was
then that my attitude changed. My fear and hatred
were taken away. Shortly after the passage was
read, we had a coffee break. I wanted to be alone.
I went upstairs. I sat down and I prayed for
openness. I prayed that God would open me to his
Spirit if it was his will. I realized later that, there
in that room I had made my act of faith. I knew that
before I could ever be "prayed over" I would have
to place my complete trust and confidence in God
and in the love of Christ and the workings of his
Spirit. I would have to accept God for himself, not
because I wanted to become again an active part
of the community. That is not what Christianity
is all about. The community is good, vital, and very
necessary in the Christian life. But if the community
does not center itself on Christ, then it is no more
than a social club that meets once a week for
bridge. The center of the community is Christ,
Christ for himself, and *then* Christ as he is made
present in the members of the community.

I realized in that room that I must first accept
God as the center of my life for himself because
he is my God, my Lord and my creator. My fear
was gone, and I went downstairs smiling for the
first time in a long time. The second part of the
prayer meeting was beautiful. Everyone there was

prayed over, including me. I remember I wasn't even afraid when I heard them speaking in tongues. Instead I was filled with joy over the visible presence of the Spirit in that room. When I was prayed over I remember being filled with an inner calm and peace that I had never felt before. There was no thunder or vision, just a beautiful peace.

We had many prayer meetings after that, but the real change within our community was the weekend prayer meeting that we had with some students from Michigan State. There were about eighty of us that weekend. So many things happened to me that weekend that it would take too long to write about them all. I was filled with a real confidence in the power of God that weekend, something that I pray I never lose. I think that it was during that weekend that I really became aware of Christ as the unifying force of the community. The love of God was so actively present in everyone there that upon entering a room one was practically struck dumb by the strong visible presence of God. The Holy Spirit was present with us all. I was filled with a courage that I never before possessed. I realized that there were many girls at St. Mary's who would want to know about this and would be just as closed and opposed as I had been. I prayed all during that weekend that I would be given God's grace to be able to bring the message of Christ to the girls there. I knew too well what kind of opposition and closedness I would receive, for I knew it would be much the same as my reaction was before receiving baptism in the Holy Spirit.

Those next few weeks were the most amazing weeks of my life. There was no one at the school with whom I could really talk except one girl who was as busy as I was talking of Christ to the students. I received open and bitter opposition from many of my closest friends. Many girls that I hardly knew would come up to me in the hall or in the cafeteria and ask me about the baptism in the Holy Spirit. Sometimes they would ask me if it were true that people were speaking in "funny" tongues—that question was the most popular. I would stay up until two and three in the morning talking to a girl; sometimes I would have to cut a class (or two or three) to finish a conversation. I had a new boldness to speak out to girls that I knew would be opposed to what I would say. Before, I could speak of God only to girls who thought practically the same way as I did about religion and faith, girls who had shared similar experiences to mine in the past two years. But now I realized that there were 1,000 other girls at school who needed Christ, who needed to be shown that he loved them, was concerned about them, and that they needed him. Those weeks were hard, because I felt very much alone in my work of spreading the word of Christ. I was receiving nothing but closed minds and attitudes, mockery and bitterness. I wasn't alone though. I wasn't alone because I had the Spirit of God's love and guidance with me. My times spent in prayer were the happiest times. I was realizing the joy of prayer. To be able to kneel down and say "I love you Lord, and I thank you for the gift of yourself." Praise of God was something I had never done before. I always prayed when I wanted something or in thanksgiving, or because I knew it was the thing every good Christian should do in order to become

closer to God and to better his life as a
Christian. Now it was joyful to pray to God in praise
of himself. I experienced an extreme closeness and
joyfulness while I prayed. Before, I was happy after
I prayed, but now the joy was coming while I
prayed. I was no longer conscious of only myself
but of God in prayer.

It wasn't all sunshine. There was a period when I
completely wanted to abandon everything and give
everything up. But God loved me too much to
let me. God made me realize man's sinfulness in a
very real and a very personal and horrifying way.
I learned much. I learned that God loves, really loves
man in a way man is incapable of understanding.
God realizes the sinfulness and the ugliness of man,
yet loves him still with a completely selfless and
undemanding love. It is man who owes God the
duty to spread his word. His word is Christ, and if I
am to call myself a Christian it is my duty as a
Christian to spread Christ's message to all. And it
is through the intercession of the Holy Spirit, it is
through his power and grace that this is carried out.
I have really experienced this and I firmly
believe this to be true.

I am not writing this to preach pentecostalism.
Those who know me well know that this is not how
I feel. I am writing this to preach Christ, to
speak about all the blessings he has given to me,
one of his sinners. He is good and has done many
wonderful things for us, his people on earth. We
have only to open our eyes to all the blessings
he has showered upon us.

I know what I have been given. And I know the
joyful obligation I have as a Christian. I still love

my beautiful friends in our community; they are still important to me. But I will say one other thing— that God is more important. He is *the* most important Person in my life. It is summer now, and I miss my friends; that is only human. But I am not miserable or desolate or horribly lonely. Because I have God; I have the Spirit of his love to guide me. I am happy to say I am joyful in the Lord, and I shall, with his grace and his love, always sing his praise and preach his word!

Bert Ghezzi

Bert Ghezzi took his B.A. from Duquesne in 1963 before going on to doctoral studies at Notre Dame. He is now an Assistant Professor of History at Grand Valley State College in Michigan.

All glory be to God the Father, through Jesus Christ. Through his wounds and by his blood he has made us a new creation.

I was born and raised a Roman Catholic. My mother, our local parish priests and the Sisters in the parish grade school grounded me in the forms of traditional Catholic piety. I was thought of and gloried in pretending to be the "model Catholic boy" all through my youth. All glory and praise was heaped on me. I reveled in it, all the while painfully aware of being phony. From childhood through college I saw myself as the center of everything: I occupied the place in my life from which Jesus ought to have reigned.

After high school I busied myself with what I

thought was Jesus' work. I tried to lead others
to him without knowing him myself. I got involved
in teaching religion for our parish Confraternity of
Christian Doctrine. I campaigned for liturgical
renewal. I helped form and lead a study-prayer-action
group at college. I dreamed I was spearheading a
revolution for Jesus. I was merely exalting myself.
I continued on this path when I enrolled in
graduate school at the University of Notre Dame.

All the while Jesus was working in me, preparing
me to embrace him. I first had an experience of
his presence and power when I was twenty. A
dear friend who has been for six years now God's
instrument for my salvation taught me how to pray.
When I first began to open to him in the winter of
1962, Jesus made himself palpably present to me,
providing me with a fleeting taste of what he had
in store for me.

But Jesus brought me to accept himself and
his Father not only through the joy of his presence.
He allowed me to be crushed under the weight
of my sin before he flooded me with his redeeming
grace. He allowed me to wallow in my conceit. He
let me slowly come to the end of my own way which
led nowhere and led me through his way.

The Lord gave me a lovely and wonderfully
patient wife and a number of wise and dedicated
friends to help me through the trials. They taught
me how to trust God. One of them (the same man
who taught me to pray and led us eventually to
baptism in the Holy Spirit) pushed me into
Jesus' arms when he chided me for being so proud
in my wickedness that I did not think Jesus' sacrifice
was enough to save me. This was a small turning

point for me. A bigger one came last October when
I prayed among a group of friends that Jesus
would accept me as I was, full of sin and helpless.

While Jesus was preparing me he was also
preparing my wife. Mary Lou is one of God's special
children. (She will not like my writing this but it is
true.) In my pride I always thought I was the strong
one bearing her up. Was I blind! Now I know why
God sent her to me and me to her, for his power
is truly glorified in her weakness. Mary Lou has
known God's holiness since childhood. She learned
to pray intimately with Jesus as a child. She has
always had a sense of living in the community of
Christ's body, always grieving when any bitterness
harmed it. She protests she is not very deep in
her spiritual life—but I'll let God be the judge
of that.

Through high school and college Jesus gently
let her grow in him bringing her aid through two or
three special friends. The gift of faith has always
been with her. Where my apostolic work was
somewhat empty and very self-centered, she did
his work humbly, both directly with Extension
Volunteers and indirectly in all her contacts.

Mary Lou and I were married in June 1964, one
year after we graduated from college. We began our
life together by putting Christ at the very center
of our marriage. That soon changed. I think now our
failure was due to the fact that we were trying to do
it ourselves without really relying on him. Our
prayer life fell apart. Both of us reached spiritual
"lows" in the past two years. Thank the Lord
Mary Lou has always been strong and patient—
she's had to bear her cross and mine too. Together

we were led through a dark valley to the light.

It was part of God's loving kindness to shower his mercy on us together as on one person. We both received the baptism in the Holy Spirit on Sunday, March 5, 1967. Our friend visited us in South Bend and prayed with us for the gift of the Spirit. I feel quite silly now recalling how frightened I was all evening while we prayed and read over some of the promises God made in the scriptures. Imagine being afraid of God's love—but I was. Our friend gently chided me again. I asked him to pray with me. Nothing dramatic or special (to the human way of looking at things) happened to me while we were praying—no thunder, no emotional outburst. I had enjoyed deeper prayer before. But the Holy Spirit took away my fear and replaced it with his peace and joy. Even so I had some trouble believing that I had received the anointing of the Holy Spirit. I thought that if the Spirit were more active in me I ought not have to force myself to believe it. I was still reluctant to step out in faith. Mary Lou was blessed with a greater faith. She received, but did not yield to, the charismatic gift of tongues that night. She resisted the charism because she wanted to be sure that she was not being deceived by her physical condition—she had delivered our second son only five days before. (Our two boys set the background for us by crying for a part of the evening in their back bedroom while we were praying in the living room.) But she was not deceived.

Again the faith of a few of my friends bore me up. Seeing that they believed that they had received baptism in the Holy Spirit, I began to believe. In less than a week's time Jesus healed me completely of the spiritual obstacle which I had struggled with for years without relief. My life has not been the same since, nor has Mary Lou's. We have truly been born anew through the blood of Jesus and through his resurrection. One week later at a prayer meeting in the home of a dear pentecostal friend, my wife yielded to and I with seven of our friends received the gift of tongues.

Mary Lou and I are twenty-seven years old. It took Jesus that long to break our stony hearts and give us hearts of flesh. But he has! Since this experience we have begun to grow in his love, in his peace and joy. His presence and his power have transformed our lives. He has given us faith.

He has given us a gift of praise and prayer. Both of us had tried for a long time to lead prayerful lives without much success. But God has begun to lead us in prayer with an ease and depth and consolation we never knew before. In moments of discouragement I have prayed and felt refreshed by his streams of living water. In moments of severe temptation, because now our sense of sin has been forcefully impressed upon us by the holiness of God's Spirit which I could not have withstood before, I have prayed and Jesus delivered me from it. Mary Lou has been more able to cast all of her cares upon Jesus. She has been given his peace as the healing antidote to her natural anxiety. When she prays in tense moments God's power is with her to see her through.

As many of our friends have discovered, the Holy Spirit has renewed our love for the Church. Where there was only the hulk of an institution for us before, we have found, life, power, and warmth. Traditional devotions such as those to Mary have become meaningful to us (and I am one who put Mary completely out of the picture many years ago). Especially the sacramental life of the Church has become more meaningful, particularly the sacrament of penance which we both use now with greater fruit than ever before.

Mary Lou and I are learning how to be witnesses for Christ. We had tried for years, but not with much success. In the past year God has made us bold. He is teaching us how to rely on Jesus to give us the words he wants us to speak. He has taught us how to witness to Jesus the Savior, instead of to ourselves.

There is so much more to praise God for. We have been blessed so richly and have witnessed so many miracles he has worked in people's lives that we can sing alleluia all our days. And it is just the beginning. Shortly after we received "baptism" I watched three Notre Dame men demonstrating to a helpless baby rabbit how to jump. Mary Lou and I feel like that rabbit. We are full of new life, and God himself has begun to teach us his ways.

A word to our friends. We have written this testimony to praise Jesus and Jesus alone. We wrote it because we know Jesus wants you to come to him and enjoy his mercy and loving kindness. We are praying that everyone who reads this will surrender to him.

Mary Pat Bradley

Mary Pat Bradley attended St. Mary's College and received an M.A. from its graduate school of theology. She is involved in many community activities and conducts a local C.C.D. teacher-training program.

A Dominican nun once asked me: "When did you come to know Christ?" I answered that I had been a Roman Catholic all my life. She rejoined "That's not what I asked you. I asked you when you first came to know Christ."

I had little difficulty answering this question. In one way or another I had been meeting and replying to such inquiry for nearly two months, in a restless, joyfully challenging effort to share Christ's mercy with others, as he had shared it unceasingly with me. After fifteen years of searching for the way in which I must love God and others while afflicted with a congenital paralytic handicap, he signed the invitation which he had been preparing and offering me for all that time. In some moments he had run after me with it—in others he had actually taken hold in an effort to place it in my possession. Always he had called with dogged but friendly insistence and awaited my reply with a mysterious urgency, almost as someone in need of my love and concern.

In carrying this story back nearly fifteen years, my purpose is to affirm the presence of Christ in every moment of crisis, as an influence—albeit through indecision, fear and uncertainty at first—upon every action, thought, desire, hope, and determination. Through fourteen months of hospital confinement, through the ensuing transition by way of high school and college, through graduate school, practice teaching and the realities consequent upon my free acceptance of the Holy Spirit's influence over specific areas of my life, Christ has been ever present, even if at first very negatively as a threat to personal security and control.

After ten years of public education, the long awaited enrollment in a Catholic high school brought promise that the nuns would be able to tell me why I was handicapped. They were not able to do so, except in the most general terms accompanied by the most firm but sympathetic exhortations to persevere as a close friend of "our suffering Savior who loved me with a special love." Encouraged by this, and given the friendship of the Sisters, I obeyed. At no time would I become deeply involved in conversation with more than one person; efforts to show concern for people seemed too small, childish, and generally useless. I wished to do something great for God—what, how, or even why, I knew not.

I entered St. Mary's College full of anticipation that my thirst for knowledge, beauty, peace, and fruitful creativity would find satisfaction. Desiring breadth and depth, determined to form friendships, and deeply resolved to communicate and to somehow make sense of my vision of things, I listened to the older teachers, met all of my instructors at the earliest moment of each term, and studied the humanities, especially theology, with incredible expectancy. As always, I feared and hated all failure, regarding myself as a burden already. I withheld involvement in school activities except to give verbal support.

Noble, stoic, emotional repression deliberately continued and intensified, since it seemed the most Christianly heroic attitude to assume. I remained unconvinced of personal usefulness, freedom, and need in many areas, and I was unable to express a sudden grasp of the relationship between physical and psychological dependence.

God, parents, three teachers, hundreds of Sisters, and other students carried me through the first summer of graduate work in theology toward my master's degree. On the strength of hunger, thirst, and a heightened fascination with mystery, I became involved in continuous dialogue with scripture. Two things emerged with absolute certainty: my need and the desire to enter fully into community and my determination to spend a lifetime if necessary in search of redemptive pain as opposed to despair and anguish. Fearing frailty, loneliness, and separation above all else, I sought their meaning in the God of the Old Testament, in the person of blind Bartimeus, and in an attempt to reconcile faith with immediate reality. Academic success, and the basic willingness of teachers and students to share these concerns, opened up a universe. Christ began to appeal to the objective basis of a friendship which would allow open dialogue and honest questioning, while at the same time my world of abstract absolutes was being pulled apart by good people. Thereafter I spent a full year and another summer in theology, finding increasing interest in people. The thesis I had long wanted to write on the distinction between anguish and suffering became reality.

The following fall brought completion of all content work and education courses required for student teaching. But of infinitely greater importance

was the entry of a Holy Cross priest with long
pastoral experience among young people into the
midst of my efforts to become real. If one must praise
God for any human friendship, one must glorify
him particularly for those which, through long
hours of dialogue, questioning, sharing, and mutual
confirmation, anticipate one's imminent opening to
the power of the Holy Spirit.

Second term plunged me into student teaching,
where the labor brought some degree of independence,
but also increased my anxious concern to find
my "niche." It was during this time that I found
myself listening fuzzily to accounts of signs and
wonders being wrought by the Holy Spirit in response
to prayers of faith. For two months I listened to
Dorothy Ranaghan, a friend and fellow teacher
at the high school. I read every word concerning
this sudden cloudburst, and became increasingly
convinced that I was seeing a (for God) perfectly
legitimate and utterly logical intervention of heaven
into the muddled affairs of earth. April, 1967,
brought my first personal involvement with a
prayer meeting at the Ranaghan home. It was a
pleasant and joyful evening, but bewildering. By
three hours after the beginning of the second
gathering, however, I had received the baptism
in the Holy Spirit, having prepared myself for the
certainty that nothing would ever be *quite* the same
again, because the gifts would shatter my introvertive
inclinations. Without emotion following the event,
but with great warmth of body and a great ease,
I invited all present to join me in the *Magnificat*.
Since the end of June I have occasionally made

use of the gift of a written tongue. I yielded after
much struggle, to a few words of speech, but seemed
to possess the written tongue in an increasing degree
of spontaneity.

Gradually, there has been an increase in
self-acceptance, clarity of motivation, willingness
to praise God and ability to take initiative and to
accept risk. Concern for the needful and ecumenical
involvement, as well as renewal of old or feared or
long dormant contacts, has increased faith, encouraged
creativity, and given much insight into weakness
as both an asset and a drawback.

This experience of communal prayer in the
spirit of the psalmist has in no way jeopardized
concern for, or participation in, the institutional life,
the sacramental realities or the traditional devotions
of the Church. Authority, liturgy, and individual
prayerful devotion have deepened in personal
and intellectual as well as in communal and spiritual
significance. A search into the inner meaning of
priesthood, teaching, and prayer occupies my mind
most of the time; no article of faith, no effort of
the Church and the world to determine moral
rectitude and the meaning of person escapes notice,
nor should it. It has become obvious that the Holy
Spirit has rendered operative all of his gifts in one
or another respect, particularly those appropriate
to the intellectual life and to patient endurance.
He has enabled me to use counsel in areas which
formerly had been to me sources of pain.

I praise God for being the Artist, the Hound,
the Friend, the Teacher, and the Healer that he

is. I praise him for following me, for interrupting
my own futility, for sending satisfaction of needs at
his pleasure to my benefit. I praise him for having
empowered me to believe in the absolute necessity
to praise and to preach the gospel of peace and
joy. I praise him for being, for creating, for
challenging the spirit of a man to open his Spirit,
until that man is left, happily, without a choice.
I praise him lastly, for being one who keeps his
promises, but who demands to enter into dialogue
with his creatures concerning them.

With God almost too much is possible! Amen!
Alleluia!

Kenneth Wolf

*Ken Wolf is a doctoral candidate in history at
Notre Dame. He is involved in many social action
and political activities.*

I believe in God. I believe in the redemptive work
of his Son Jesus Christ. I believe that Christ loves
me personally and that he is actively helping me
to realize this love—its power and ubiquitousness
—in all my daily life through the action of his
Holy Spirit.

This is a simple act of faith, similar in form to
ones that abound in Roman Catholic liturgy and are
memorized by every grade schooler. Yet four months
ago I could not have written these words with the
conviction that I now possess. Now entering my
nineteenth year of formal education, I have for
some years shared the interests common to my
generation. I prided myself on my attempt to seek

rational solutions to my personal problems and hoped some day to use this ability to aid my fellow man. However, alongside this vague but sincere humanitarian rationalist who gloried in his ability to meet the challenges that had come his way, existed an all-too-real creature of great human frailty beset by serious emotional problems and increasingly frustrated by his inability to solve these problems by human means. The marriage of conscientious idealism and human weakness—one that many of us contract—cannot last. Under the guise of a process often known as "maturation," most of us divorce ("separate" is perhaps a better word for this gradual act) our ideals. Our marriage of convenience fails on the rocks of "reality."

But is this reality? My weaknesses were real and so was my failure to conquer them. Yet, the only ultimately real factor in the human situation— Almighty God—had been foolishly left out. God was not dead; I was simply indifferent to him and to his real power to help me. My infrequent prayers for help in moments of extreme crisis lacked any sustained effort. I was not a convinced Christian.

This is no longer the case. I had for long been convinced of my own weaknesses. I am now convinced that I no longer have to bear these alone, and indeed that these very weaknesses can be turned into strengths. For this I give heartfelt and joyous testimony to the saving power of Jesus Christ and his Almighty Father manifested through the action of the Holy Spirit in my own life.

When my wife and I first heard about the movement of the Holy Spirit at Notre Dame we were respectful—perhaps only because Bert Ghezzi, the intermediary that God had used to tell us was a person that we both deeply respected. For several weeks we thought about what he had told us: about the fruits of the Spirit, especially peace, patience, joy and love, which had changed his life and those of many other people around Notre Dame; about the charismatic gifts of the Spirit, speaking in tongues, prophecy, interpretation and healing, which had become operative in our fellow students; about these people who were mightily in word and deed proclaiming the power of God in the 20th century. We thought, and tried to pray—reading the Acts of the Apostles—about all this that seemed to be too good to be true, but apparently was. I was bothered most by the diminution of the human intellect and will that this submission to the power of God seemed to imply. This reservation was an intellectual one, but it was, I now realize, strongly influenced by human pride; could I admit that God could do for me what I had not been able to do for myself?

Then one evening my wife and I found our usual after dinner chit-chat opening into a full-blown mutual examination of conscience. We found that many of our problems—from long-range dissatisfaction with ourselves to the daily vexations of married life —were rooted in this sin of pride. After a four-hour conversation, one of the frankest of our married life, we prayed, opened our bible to the Book of Sirach and found there a terribly appropriate message that condemned pride but provided the most comforting alternative: "For gold is tested in the

fire, and acceptable men in the furnace of
humiliation. Trust in him, and he will help you;
make your ways straight, and hope in him. You who
fear the Lord, wait for his mercy" (Sir. 2, 5-7).

The following night we attended our first prayer
meeting and received the laying on of hands and
the baptism in the Holy Spirit. Our lives truly
have been changed. A great problem has been lifted
from me. I have also found perseverance in the
arduous task of study imposed on a graduate student.
With each passing week, my entire perspective on life
has become less egocentric and more Christocentric.

I am slowly developing the kind of faith Christ
speaks of in Mark (11, 24) when he tells his
followers: "Therefore I tell you, whatever you
ask in prayer, believe that you receive it and
you will."

The Spirit has given (and is continuing to give)
both my wife and me the ability to pray and to love
each other in a way we couldn't have done before.
Above all, he has given us faith and the ability
and willingness to confidently claim the graces that
the Son of God won for us by his death. We are,
indeed, surprisingly free with our requests for divine
aid in our daily life. Our confidence in God and our
desire and ability to call on him are our own
humble form of praise of the Father. I wish more
than ever to do God's work in the world. Because
I now realize my dependence upon God, my human
nature is being fulfilled not destroyed, my weaknesses
are becoming strengths. Because I now realize the
emptiness of human success in itself, I am offering
my present and future success to the Father to be
used in spreading the joy of the Lord and the praise

of his power and goodness. Years of frustration and self-doubt are being ended by a simple "I believe."

Mrs. John Orth

Mrs. John Orth is a widow and a mother who works at a Catholic hospital in Elwood, Indiana.

"Come Holy Spirit." And he did! And now I am alive again. For a long time I felt I was a Christian. I attended Mass and the sacraments regularly, did parish work and tried to be kind and helpful to my friends and neighbors even though I had my share of suffering. Seven members of my family died in one year's time. My husband after a year of much suffering with cancer, and my sister killed instantly in an auto accident. I was very bitter. Then through the love of my son and other friends I began to see our "Father's" love again.

However, I felt there was something else, something deeper, but I couldn't put my finger on just what it was I needed. I kept searching—and you might say yearning—but "it" was just out of my reach. The trouble was with *me,* I knew. Then I was taken to Notre Dame to a prayer meeting. My son Philip had heard Ralph Martin speak at St. Meinrad's, and when Philip came home for the summer we decided to go to take some friends to a prayer meeting. There I found what I was looking for —the Holy Spirit which I had received at confirmation but didn't fully realize until this night when hands were laid on me and I was prayed with and I finally stripped myself of all my pride and false Christianity. It came hard because I had held back, but praise God it wracked the depths of my soul with deep sobs and I couldn't have held back if I wanted to. I felt free, clean and a new person and completely filled with the Holy Spirit. I didn't ask for any special gift, just to be filled with his Spirit. Two weeks later I went back to Notre Dame not for myself, but I thought to go to pray for someone else. It was at this prayer meeting that I was given the gift of speaking in tongues to praise God the Father. I also have received a love of the scripture that I never had before. My day is not complete unless I read the word of God. My deep awareness of the Mass has increased, and my love and understanding of our clergy have also increased. I could go on and on but all I want to say is "praise God for all eternity and thank him."

Philip Orth

Phil Orth received his B.A. from St. Meinrad's College and is currently teaching in an inner-city school in Scranton, Pennsylvania.

I wish to tell you of the new life that I have experienced this past summer and am continuing, through God's grace, to experience with the passing of each new day. The words I write are not my own words so much as his, as he dictates them to me for you through the impulse of his Holy Spirit. Listen, and hear now, as you read, what God has done for me.

On a visit to St. Meinrad Seminary in southern Indiana in 1968, I became quite taken up with news of a seemingly radical new movement in the Church coming out of Pittsburgh, East Lansing, and Notre Dame. A young layman came down to St. Meinrad's from East Lansing to tell us of it during the course of a recollection he was giving us. The new movement (at least it sounded new to our day and age) centers around the belief in the tangible coming of the Holy Spirit into the lives of any who ask in complete and unhesitating faith, complete with all the gifts of the Holy Spirit as mentioned in St. Paul (1 Cor. 12). It didn't take long at all to see that this young man was possessed with an inner life that wasn't a bit phony or put on, but which seemed almost imperceptibly to beam from him and penetrate into you. By the end of the recollection I knew I had to find out more about this more complete life in Christ through his Holy Spirit. I thought I had known a fairly intimate relationship with the Lord previously through my Cursillo, but nothing so tangible and powerful as this pentecostal renewal had been described.

I came home from school in May and told my mother and several others in our community about this new movement of the Holy Spirit into the Church. Many seemed interested in learning more about it. So a group of us went up to Notre Dame one Saturday evening to the campus where they hold prayer meetings. In these meetings the Holy Spirit was invoked to make his divine presence in our lives more manifest in order that the Father might be more glorified in and through us. There were approximately 150 of us gathered in a very compact mass inside an average size classroom, and I would say that the majority of those present were nuns.

The evening began with an explanation of just what it was we were all gathered together to do that night, the relevance of what we were about, and its scriptural and theological validity. This was all given by a grad student there at Notre Dame in the school of theology, and was followed up by a number of others from the faculty and the student body there at Notre Dame. They all gave their testimony to the fact that there was no doubt in their minds but that they had received in recent weeks the fullness of their confirmation, or, in the words of the first Christians, they had received the full awareness of their baptism in the Holy Spirit. They did not hesitate to make known that along with this greater awareness they had received many of the gifts of the Holy Spirit, including healing, prophecy, greatly increased faith, tongues, and the interpretation of tongues. I sat there all ears to everything being said, hope increasing all the time that this was all really possible.

As the evening went on, there was singing, spontaneous praying out loud, scripture reading, and more sharing of the things God had done in the lives of the various ones there. It was all conducted on a very free-flowing, unplanned, spontaneous basis, and was punctuated very heavily with extended periods of silence in which I prayed very hard that God would send his Holy Spirit in his fullness to us and pour out his miraculous gifts upon us so that we might be made stronger, and purer, and more beautiful witnesses of his presence and his love. One could feel the intensity of the concentration in the room, and, oh, the songs were so expressive and so filling.

After about an hour and a half, Father Edward O'Connor, the Holy Cross priest at Notre Dame so involved in this movement, stood up in the midst of the assembly and suggested that we take a break for a few minutes in order to rest our prayerful souls and our cramped bodies. He then went on to announce that anyone who wished to could be prayed with and have hands laid on him in either one of the two smaller classrooms across the hall. I got up and went into one of the smaller classrooms thinking to myself that I might as well go all the way—get the whole treatment—if I was to honestly and fairly evaluate this movement for myself. After all, that was my entire reason for coming to the prayer meeting; to come and see for myself and to experience if I could, all that had been coming to me recently concerning this renewal among some of our Catholic brothers of the power of the Holy Spirit.

As I entered the room we (about twenty-five of us) were asked to sit down in desks that were arranged for us in rows. Those who had already received this greatly heightened awareness of their baptism in the Holy Spirit previous to this occasion were standing at the front of the room praying and listening as one from among them gave a brief explanation to us of what was about to take place. An emphatic warning was sounded that we should not expect any great emotional kick at the moment that we were being prayed with, but that on the other hand if it should be given to us to pray aloud (in tongues or otherwise), or to cry, to sing, or whatever, we should feel free to give vent to it, and it would be a visible sign to all, though not a necessary one, that God is moving in us through his Holy Spirit, for the Spirit comes in a variety of ways. A prayer was then offered exorcising the devil from each one of us and from the entire room, and then they came forward in groups of threes and fours. Laying their hands upon each of us individually, they prayed with us as a gesture of fraternal charity that we, too, might receive, then and there, the full awareness of our confirmation, our baptism in the Holy Spirit.

As they prayed over me, I let my mind go blank so as to make for free access of the Holy Spirit. I was being extremely cautious that anything which might come be from God and not from me. They finished, three of them having prayed in tongues over me. I felt nothing. As far as I was concerned, nothing had happened. So, becoming more and more convinced that something could and should happen as some sort of a sign that the Father had sent his Holy Spirit more fully into me, I literally yelled out amidst the others in the room: "Dammit Jesus, why are you so damn abstract?" It was a very audible witness before God and men that I was asking God for help and for life, that I needed him (and I did) desperately! They came to me and asked me if I'd mind if they prayed with me again. Of course I consented and that second time I knew God was working within me. I could feel a distinct tingling in my hands, and immediately I became bathed in a hard sweat that seemed to pop out of every pore. Also, at that moment, a word came into my mind that I cannot ever recall hearing

before—*Rasheim*. However, the most beautiful
and the most enduring phenomenon that was given
me then, and has been with me ever since, is a
gift that seems to be the common experience of all
who, through an initial leap of faith, have received
this greater fullness of the Holy Spirit in their lives.
The gift I speak of is the gift of a deep and abiding
peace. Deep down inside me that night I could feel
it being planted, and ever since then it has grown
considerably and brought me into a communion
with God that I had never begun to know previously.
It has risen within me to long periods (several hours)
of near ecstasy in which I'd swear I was experiencing
a foretaste of the Kingdom of Heaven, and then has
subsided again into "normalcy," though always
enduring and never completely leaving.

It was only a beginning. Since then the Lord
has been making his presence in my life—my new
life—known more and more in many various ways
that have at times astounded me with his truly
saving power. For example, for the first time in my
life I had a real desire to read scripture. In fact, I
happened to be in bed the following night after my
Notre Dame experience when all of a sudden I had
this terrific urge to pray and to read scripture, and
not just any old thing in scripture either. I felt
that for some unknown reason I just had to turn to
second Timothy, and I had never read second
Timothy before in my life. This was about 1 A.M.
I prayed for a little while and then began reading
from this text. All of a sudden I came across a passage
that really hit me between the eyes: "They will keep
up the outer appearances of religion, but will have
rejected the inner power of it" (2 Tim. 3, 5). The

verse was a part of a prophecy Paul was making to
Timothy. I asked myself whether we had been
rejecting the inner power of the Lord. How have we
long scoffed at and made fun of those who in our
day and age claim to speak in other languages they
themselves cannot understand while praying, or who
have really gone mad and claimed to have been healed
or to have healed someone through prayer. How
many times have I heard it said by dignitaries in my
own Roman Catholic Church that miracles of this
personal nature should be discouraged among the
faithful today, that the Church no longer needs
to rely on them as they did in the first century.
I knew right then and there that the Lord was
talking about me and my generation as well as the
many generations that have preceded mine which
have for the most part rejected the power of the
Lord. This scriptural message, as well as many
others which the Lord has drawn me to, spoke to
me in a deeply personal way like never before. No
longer do I read the word of God as though its words
and events were meant only for those people living
2,000 years ago. I now know that it is a forever
living word which speaks personally to men and
every man of every generation, for I have known
the experience of its deep personal message to me.
I might at this point add also that the Mass has
become much more meaningful and personal to me
also since having received this infusion of new life.

On the night I came home from summer school
and my first prayer meeting, my mother was suddenly
awakened around 2.30 A.M. because I was talking
very loudly in my sleep. She said she thought
I was awake and praying from the way it sounded;

only the words I was using were not in English.
She stated that I was praying in tongues using very
loud and distinct syllables. Her room is just across
a small hallway from mine and both our doors were
open. She said I was talking so loudly that I could
have been heard all over the house. I found out
nothing about the incident until the next day when
she asked me about it, still thinking that I had
been wide awake talking to myself throughout the
entire experience. One point she stressed was that
what I said that night was not the usual
mumbo-jumbo of someone talking in his sleep.
The words she heard were very precise and distinct,
and she was positive, without a doubt, that it sounded
like a foreign language to her. It was big news to
me when she told me about it, and we both praised
God for his graciousness. Two weeks later on a
Sunday morning I found myself consciously praying
to the Lord in a foreign tongue, and I have
continued doing this nearly every day since.

I feel I must add a word of comment about
these tongues that I have just reported receiving. We
read in many places throughout the New Testament
of this phenomenon occurring with many different
people, always as the direct result of having received
baptism in the Holy Spirit that both Jesus and
St. Paul speak of many times. I, personally, found
it a very difficult thing to open myself up to, and
for several weeks following my renewed baptism in
the Spirit at Notre Dame, I literally fought the thing
tooth and nail. People who had also received
this heightened renewal of their confirmation were
telling me that I could speak in tongues if I only
believed and gave it a chance. So, occasionally, I

attempted praying in tongues when alone, and every time, I became quite disgusted with it, with the whole thing, because I felt that as far as I was concerned it was me doing this, not God. When it did finally come, I knew it was God and not me, and I gave free reign to it in front of others as well as in private. Where before only disgust with myself came of it, now a beautiful peace and confidence accompanied it, a heightening, that is, of that initial peace which has endured.

You may ask of what practical use is it to be able to speak in another language to God, one that you have no idea yourself as to what it means. I have found its value to lie in the totality and quality it adds to my prayer, especially in my prayers of praise to God. You've known times in your own life, I'm sure, when words just don't seem adequate enough to express what you really feel you want to say.

In conclusion, I want to say that this recent outpouring of the Holy Spirit—to any and to all who wish to submit their entire lives to Christ, who believe Christ meant literally what he said in Mark 16, 17-18 or in John 14, 11-14—is not new. It's something that's been with us ever since Christ has. The only really new things about it are the people who have opened themselves up to the full power and love of God in their lives.

3

Roots of the Baptism
in the Holy Spirit

> "We are not pentecostals... We are Catholics who have had a pentecostal experience... a deepened experience of the Holy Spirit."
>
> *The National Catholic Reporter*

It is strange, this story of Catholic "pentecostalism." Here are found elements so desired: spiritual awakening, renewal of communities of Christians, deeper faith-life; and things so odd: speaking in tongues, claims of visions, prophecy and healing. Is it possible to give theological room to this charismatic collage in the rich mosaic of Christian life? Just by itself, prescinding from its cultural context, a theology of life in the Spirit, accompanied by continual charismatic experience, poses many difficult questions. But in the total picture of what is going on about us—of where pentecostalism has come from, of where renewal in the Church is going, of all the ecumenical and intra-Church tensions in today's Christianity—the Catholic pentecostal movement must be critically examined from a number of standpoints. Those who give testimony to it are going to have to take a deep breath before trying to explain themselves.

Certainly it is too early to attempt a definitive explanation of the "pentecostal experience," yet normal and reasonable theological questions must be faced and answered. How does pentecostalism fit with the teaching and practice of the Catholic Church? Are Catholic pentecostals, for want of a better term, presuming to impart the Holy Spirit? Do we not receive the Spirit in baptism and confirmation? How does it relate to the liturgical life of the Church? If it has a good purpose why haven't we heard about it before now? And why should it happen today? These are some of the questions we shall approach in the next two chapters, fully aware that what is said here is not all that could be said and that much further investigation must follow.

The Work of the Holy Spirit in the New Testament

In trying to assess the value of something like pentecostalism, we should turn first to the testimony of the inspired word of God, written under the guidance of the Holy Spirit by the Christian community. Then we should turn to the history, theology, and liturgical practice of the Church for further explanation.

The New Testament was composed in, by, and for the community of believers. Gathered together by a common experience of new life in Christ, the first Christians often talked about Jesus and about the meaning of his life, death, resurrection, and his sending of the Spirit back into the new Church. They remembered his teachings and the deeds of his life which they now understood more fully than in the days when the Lord had walked among them. With this deeper understanding they began to set down in writing the faith-story of the "Christ event." Themselves filled with the Spirit since the day of Pentecost, the evangelists and later the writers of the epistles proclaimed their beliefs about the work of the Spirit of the Lord among them.

In the New Testament the reception of the Holy Spirit is often related to some concrete function or service an individual was called on to perform for the People of God. In the Gospel according to St. Luke we see John the Baptist's career predicted: "... he will be filled with the Holy Spirit, even from his mother's womb. And he will turn many of the sons of Israel to the Lord their God ... to make ready for the Lord a people prepared" (Lk. 1, 15-17). Shortly thereafter Mary received the Holy Spirit precisely for the function of being the mother of Jesus. "The Holy Spirit will come upon you and the power of the Most High will overshadow you; therefore the child to be born will be called holy, the Son of God" (Lk. 1, 35). Again, Elizabeth received the Spirit and immediately prophesied to Mary: "... and Elizabeth was filled with the Holy Spirit and she exclaimed with a loud cry, 'Blessed are you among women and blessed is the fruit of your womb'" (Lk. 1, 41-42).

Finally Zechariah, the father of John the Baptist, was filled with the Holy Spirit for the purpose of prophesying about his son and his son's ministry. It is interesting to note that in each of the cases in this one chapter of scripture, St. Luke, who in all probability wrote the account of Pentecost Sunday in Acts 2, links being filled with the Holy Spirit to some function, service, office, or ministry.

In Luke 3, John the Baptist is asked if he is the expected Christ; but he answers them: "I baptize you with water; but he who is mightier than I is

coming ... he will baptize you with the Holy Spirit
and with fire" (Lk. 3, 16). When Jesus comes to the
Jordan and throws in his lot with sinners by being
baptized for repentance, the Holy Spirit is seen
coming upon him (Lk. 3, 21-22) and then he is
spoken of as "full of the Holy Spirit" (Lk. 4, 1) and
as "in the power of the Spirit" (Lk. 4, 14). Of
course, this manifestation of Jesus being full of the
Holy Spirit points to and inaugurates the whole of
his public ministry. Jesus himself tells why and to
what purpose he is filled with the Holy Spirit, quot-
ing Isaiah 61, 1-2; 58, 6: "The Spirit of the Lord is
upon me because he has anointed me to preach good
news to the poor. He has sent me to proclaim release
to the captives and recovering of sight to the blind, to
set at liberty those who are oppressed, to proclaim the
acceptable year of the Lord" (Lk. 4, 18-19).

Up to this point we have seen some examples of
members of the People of God, including Jesus himself, filled with the Spirit as individuals in order to
fulfill the vocation appointed to them by the Father.
Note too that these events take place before the
death and resurrection of Jesus and before the formation of the Church as the Body of Christ.

The Holy Spirit in the New Testament Church

The summit of the earthly life of Jesus is his
paschal mystery in which, through the events of the
last supper, the passion and death of Jesus, his
resurrection-ascension, and Pentecost, the plan of
redemption is accomplished. Contemporary theology,
impelled by modern developments in the study of
scripture, liturgy and the Fathers of the Church, is

exploring anew the depths of meaning and significance of these events. The work of theologians from all over the world is renewing our appreciation and understanding of the paschal mystery.

When we look back to the last supper and Calvary today, we see the man Jesus, filled with divine power as the Son of God, obediently fulfilling the will of his Father through the most tremendous act of love in the history of the human race. Jesus loved the Father as no fallen man could ever love him. In Jesus' human response to the call of the Father there is established the perfect interpersonal relationship between God and man. God had created man to share fully in the divine life of love and now for the first time, in the humanity of Jesus, that full sharing of a man in God's life was realized. Yet Jesus was not acting as an individual, or in and for himself, but he was acting as one representing all. For he had accepted fully the weakness, anguish, and suffering of the human condition. Bearing the sinfulness of man, he accepted the ultimate consequence of man's life of estrangement from God: death. And because in life and death he so fully loved and committed himself to the will of his Father, in dying he slew death and came into the newness of life. For the Father, accepting the sacrifice of his Son, raised him up in the fullness of a perfected humanity and established him absolutely as Christ and Lord. Thus, the bonds of man's alienation from God were broken and the age-old power of Satan over man crushed, as Jesus, through shedding his blood for all, came into new life for all.

From the moment of the last supper onward, there is a renewed emphasis by Jesus on the work of the

Holy Spirit. He makes it clear to his disciples that the time is approaching when he will no longer be with them in the way to which they are accustomed. In John's gospel, Jesus' discourse at the last supper speaks of the fulfillment of the paschal mystery among the believing community in terms of mutual service and commitment as seen in the washing of the feet (Jn. 13, 5-16), of the new commandment to love one another as Jesus loved them (Jn. 13, 34-35), of the abiding presence of Jesus' power in the midst of those who believe in him (Jn. 14, 12-14), of the reality of living in Christ's love, sharing his love for the Father (Jn. 14, 18-24), of the unity of the Church in Christ in the symbol of the vine and the branches (Jn. 15, 1-10), and of the persecution that will befall those faithful to Jesus (Jn. 16, 1-4). These characteristics of the life of the Church are presented in the context of the twofold movement of Jesus going away to be glorified, to be with his Father, and of Jesus and the Father sending back the Holy Spirit into the body of believers. Throughout the discourse, this new life of the Church is linked up with the coming of the Holy Spirit.

"If you love me you will keep my commandments. And I will pray the Father, and he will give you another Counselor to be with you forever, even the Spirit of truth, whom the world cannot receive, because it neither sees him nor knows him; you know him, for he dwells with you and will be in you" (Jn. 14, 15-17).

"These things I have spoken to you while I am still with you. But the Counselor, the Holy Spirit, whom the Father will send in my name, he will teach you all things, and bring to your remembrance all that I have said to you" (Jn. 14, 25-26).

"But when the Counselor comes, whom I shall send to you from the Father, even the Spirit of truth, who proceeds from the Father, he will bear witness to me; and you also are witnesses, because you have been with me from the beginning" (Jn. 15, 26-27).

"It is to your advantage that I go away, for if I do not go away the Counselor will not come to you; but if I go, I will send him to you. And when he comes, he will convince the world of sin and of righteousness and of judgment: of sin, because they do not believe in me; of righteousness, because I go to the Father, and you will see me no more; of judgment, because the ruler of this world is judged.

"I have yet many things to say to you, but you cannot bear them now. When the Spirit of truth comes, he will guide you into all the truth; for he will not speak on his own authority, but whatever he hears he will speak, and he will declare to you the things that are to come. He will glorify me, for he will take what is mine and declare it to you. All that the Father has is mine; therefore I said that he will take what is mine and declare it to you" (Jn. 16, 7-15).

No one would maintain that we have in this one section of scripture a complete picture of the meaning of the paschal mystery for the life of the Church or a definitive description of the Church. But it can certainly be seen that the Holy Spirit is the key to the new faith-life of the Christian community after Jesus goes to the Father. The life, ministry, holiness, and suffering of Christ live on in his Church by the power of the Holy Spirit. This is the promise of Jesus to his Church.

We can find three texts in the New Testament which indicate Jesus' paschal sending of his Spirit to enliven the first Christian community: once from the cross, once on the evening of Easter Sunday, and again fifty days later on Pentecost.

The first case is found in John 19, 30; "When Jesus had received the vinegar he said 'It is finished'; and he bowed his head and gave up his spirit." It has recently been pointed out that the same text could be rendered "he handed on the Spirit." We should not be surprised at this because it is typical of St. John to compress all the events of the paschal mystery in literary forms and allusions placed at the time of Jesus' death, because the cross is so central in the mystery of salvation. The ambivalence of the text lies in the fact that Jesus gave up his life on the cross and that through his death on the cross he sent the Holy Spirit on the Church.

It is also in the gospel of John that we see Jesus bestowing the Holy Spirit on the Church on Easter Sunday evening. As soon as Jesus appeared to his disciples he greeted them in peace, showing them his hands and side. Then Jesus said: "'As the Father has sent me, even so I send you.' And when he had said this, he breathed on them, and said to them, 'Receive the Holy Spirit. If you forgive the sins of any, they are forgiven; if you retain the sins of any they are retained'" (Jn. 20, 20-23).

There are several points about this text to be made clear:

(1) The sending of the Spirit by Jesus is consequent to his resurrection and follows closely after his instruction to Mary Magdalen to tell the brethren "I am ascending to my Father and your Father, to my God and your God." Thus the Johannine theme follows the same pattern as we shall find in Luke's account of Pentecost: the sending of the Spirit is an act of the risen glorified Lord Jesus. (Contemporary theology sees the ascension and glorification of Jesus as an Easter day event, that is, on Easter day Jesus goes to the Father and is fully with the Father, while at the same time repeatedly appearing to his disciples. According to this view Ascension day marks the end of Jesus' post-resurrection appearances and indicates the expectation of the whole Church for the new Christ life in the Holy Spirit.)

(2) The reception of the Holy Spirit is closely connected with the commission or ministry of the disciples to be sent as Jesus had been sent by the Father. Thus by the power of the Holy Spirit, the primitive Church is meant to be the continuation in the world of Jesus' ministry.

(3) The reception of the Holy Spirit is closely related to the power and function to forgive sin. Clearly the forgiveness of sin, the reconciliation of man to God and man to man is the whole purpose of the incarnation, death and resurrection of Jesus. The continuation of that same redeeming ministry is transmitted to the Church. The text has two levels of meaning: first, forgiveness of sin in terms of reconciliation, binding and loosing within the Christian community, and secondly, forgiveness of sin in the sense of the preaching and communication of the

saving love of Christ through the sacramentality of the Church.

In summary, this passage talks about the vital functions of the Church and what its ministry is to do. The key to the whole project is Jesus' bestowal of the Holy Spirit on his disciples.

The third text in the New Testament which indicates Jesus' paschal sending of his Spirit to enliven the first Christian community is the account of Pentecost Sunday found in Acts 2. The Acts of the Apostles is generally attributed to St. Luke whose remarks on the Holy Spirit we have already observed. Luke, it seems, employs an historical chronology of events rather than John's style of compression as he depicts the outpouring of the Holy Spirit on the primitive Church.

In Acts 1 we read that while Jesus was with his followers after his resurrection "he charged them not to depart from Jerusalem, but to wait for the promise of the Father, which he said, 'you heard from me, for John baptized with water, but before many days you shall be baptized with the Holy Spirit ... You shall receive power when the Holy Spirit has come upon you; and you shall be my witnesses in Jerusalem and in all Judea and Samaria and to the end of the earth'" (Acts 1, 4-5. 8). After saying this, Jesus ascended into heaven. Note again that according to Jesus the result of being baptized with the Holy Spirit is the reception of power—power to witness to Christ, to preach the Gospel effectively throughout the world. In obedience to Jesus' instruction the first Christians returned to the upper room in Jerusalem where they stayed together in prayer. They were gathered in faith, concerned with each other and the inner life of their community; they did not carry on any apostolic activity.

"When the day of Pentecost had come, they were all together in one place. And suddenly a sound came from heaven like the rush of a mighty wind, and it filled all the house where they were sitting. And there appeared to them tongues as of fire, distributed and resting on each one of them. And they were all filled with the Holy Spirit and began to speak in other tongues, as the Spirit gave them utterance.

"Now there were dwelling in Jerusalem Jews, devout men from every nation under heaven. And at this sound the multitude came together, and they were bewildered, because each one heard them speaking in his own language. And they were amazed and wondered saying, 'Are not all these who are speaking Galileans? And how is it that we hear each of us in his own language? Parthians and Medes and Elamites and residents of Mesopotamia, Judea and Cappadocia, Pontus and Asia, Phrygia and Pamphylia, Egypt and the parts of Libya belonging to Cyrene, and visitors from Rome, both Jews and proselytes, Cretans and Arabians, we hear them telling in our own tongues the mighty works of God.' And all were amazed and perplexed, saying to one another, 'What does this mean?' But others mocking said, 'They are filled with new wine.'

"But Peter, standing with the eleven, lifted up his voice and addressed them, 'Men of Judea and all who dwell in Jerusalem, let this be known to you, and give ear to my words. For these men are not drunk, as you suppose, since it is only the third hour of the day; but this is what was spoken by the prophet Joel:

And in the last days it shall be, God declares
that I will pour out my Spirit upon all flesh,
and your sons and your daughters shall prophesy,
and your young men shall see visions,
and your old men shall dream dreams;
yea, and on my menservants and my maidservants
    in those days
I will pour out my Spirit; and they shall
    prophesy.
And I will show wonders in the heaven above
and signs on the earth beneath, blood, fire,
    and vapor of smoke;
the sun shall be turned into darkness and the
    moon into blood,
before the day of the Lord comes, the great and
    manifest day.
And it shall be that whoever calls on the name of
    the Lord shall be saved.

"'Men of Israel, hear these words: Jesus of Nazareth, a man attested to you by God with mighty works and wonders and signs which God did through him in your midst, as you yourselves know—this Jesus, delivered up according to the definite plan and foreknowledge of God, you crucified and killed by the hands of lawless men. But God raised him up, having loosed the pangs of death, because it was not possible for him to be held by it. For David says concerning him,

I saw the Lord always before me,
for he is at my right hand that I may not be
    shaken;
therefore my heart was glad, and my tongue
    rejoiced;
moreover my flesh will dwell in hope.
For thou wilt not abandon my soul to Hades,
nor let thy Holy One see corruption.

Thou hast made known to me the ways of life;
that wilt make me full of gladness with thy
  presence.

"'Brethren, I may say to you confidently of the
patriarch David that he died and was buried, and his
tomb is with us to this day. Being therefore a prophet,
and knowing that God had sworn with an oath to
him that he would set one of his descendants upon his
throne, he foresaw and spoke of the resurrection of
the Christ, that he was not abandoned to Hades, nor
did his flesh see corruption. This Jesus God raised up,
and of that we all are witnesses. Being therefore exalted at the right hand of God, and having received
from the Father the promise of the Holy Spirit, he has
poured out this which you see and hear. For David
did not ascend into the heavens; but he himself says,

The Lord said to my Lord, Sit at my right hand,
till I make thy enemies a stool for thy feet.

"'Let all the house of Israel therefore know assur-
edly that God has made him both Lord and Christ,
this Jesus whom you crucified.'

"Now when they heard this they were cut to the
heart, and said to Peter and the rest of the apostles,
'Brethren, what shall we do?' And Peter said to them,
'Repent, and be baptized every one of you in the name
of Jesus Christ for the forgiveness of your sins; and
you shall receive the gift of the Holy Spirit. For the
promise is to you and to your children and to all that
are far off, every one whom the Lord our God calls to
him.' And he testified with many other words and
exhorted them, saying, 'Save yourselves from this
crooked generation.' So those who received his word

were baptized, and there were added that day about
three thousand souls. And they devoted themselves
to the apostles' teaching and fellowship, to the breaking of bread and the prayers.

"And fear came upon every soul; and many wonders and signs were done through the apostles. And
all who believed were together and had all things in
common; and they sold their possessions and goods
and distributed them to all, as any had need. And
day by day, attending the temple together and breaking bread in their homes, they partook of food with
glad and generous hearts, praising God and having
favor with all the people. And the Lord added to their
number day by day those who were being saved"
(Acts 2).

In St. Luke's account this is the fulfillment of the
promise of the Holy Spirit made by Jesus in Acts 1.
We may call attention to several points:

(1) The heart of the chapter is that the primitive
Church is filled with Spirit, and consequent to that
event, for the first time after the resurrection, the
gospel is publicly preached with such power and
attraction that a vast number is converted to Christ
and initiated into the Church. It is clear that the new
dynamic power in the Church is the Holy Spirit.

(2) The coming of the Spirit is accompanied by
and attested to by several corporeal, i.e., sensible
phenomena—the sound of a rushing wind, the appear-
ance of fire-like tongues, and the disciples themselves
speaking in other than their normal language at the
prompting of the Holy Spirit.

(3) It is the speaking in tongues which attracts
attention. The scene seems to be one of raucous
exclamation rather than restrained discourse. Those

who hear this strange speaking, often called Babel in reverse, are affected in two ways. A number of foreigners understand the languages spoken by the Christians and hear of the mighty works of God; while others have the impression from the excitability of the Christians as well as from their unintelligible speech that they are drunk.

(4) Peter, assuming his role of leadership, publicly begins his first preaching. First he assures his hearers that his friends are really quite sober, which reinforces our impression that a large segment of the crowd did not understand the tongues, and secondly he attests that this strange phenomenon is the work of the Spirit of God, and in Acts 2 he quotes Joel 2, 28-32.

(5) Having claimed that he and his friends are filled with the Holy Spirit, he preaches the good news of what God had done through Jesus of Nazareth, who is Christ and Lord and sender of the Holy Spirit.

(6) The large number moved to conversion by the experience of the power of Christ is led to repent, to be baptized in Jesus' name for forgiveness of sins, and thus receive the gift of the Holy Spirit. As a result of this initiation they entered into the life of the primitive Church characterized by catechesis from the apostles, a common life of fellowship and love, the breaking of the bread, a simple eucharistic celebration, and the life of prayer. Note that through this ministry of the Spirit-filled Church, the Lord added to their number day by day those who were being saved. Thus Pentecost is not a one-day experience but a continuing reality. Because the Holy Spirit had come upon the Church and enlivened it, it became the Mystical Body of Christ, the continuation of Christ's

paschal mystery in space and time throughout history. Thus when the ministry of Christians brought sinners to conversion, St. Luke says that in reality it was the action of the risen Lord Jesus working in and through his body, the Church.

These three New Testament texts indicate the reality and purpose of Jesus sending his Spirit upon the Church. The Spirit is clearly the soul of the Church. Because the Spirit of Jesus dwells in the Church it is truly the Body of Christ. Only because it is enlivened by the Spirit can the Church continue to celebrate the paschal mystery of Christ in word and sacrament, making present and effective in each generation the fullness of redemption. Only because of the operation of the Spirit in the Church can any man become a part of Jesus, share in his sonship and through him love and worship the Father. Only in the power of the Spirit can the Christian manifest the love of Christ to others, speak out in word and deed the good news of salvation and draw men to life eternal. Without the event of Pentecost, and the ongoing reality of Pentecost, there is no Church and there is no Christian life. Salvation through Christ would then become a mere historical event, inaccessible to contemporary man.

The subject of the role of the Holy Spirit in the life of the New Testament Church is far too great to be fully approached in a work such as this. In a later chapter we will discuss some aspects of the subject in examining the gifts and fruits of the Spirit. But before we leave our present consideration of the New Testament we should examine the continuing process of Jesus bestowing or baptizing in the Holy Spirit through the ministry of the first Christian community.

The questions we turn to are: How did Christian converts receive the Holy Spirit, and what effect did the reception have?

The New Testament evidence is clear on the point that people receive the Holy Spirit by being converted to Christ and entering into the life of the Christian community. The rite used for Christian initiation was baptism. Peter gives the following directions to those touched by his preaching, "Repent and be baptized every one of you in the name of Jesus for the forgiveness of your sins, and you shall receive the gift of the Holy Spirit" (Acts 2, 38).

The religious practice of baptizing was not the creation of the apostolic Church. Purification rites, ritual washings and baptism were very much a part of the cultic and social practice of that age. We have already seen that John the Baptist employed immersion in water as a symbol of repentence. There are other records of Jewish proselyte baptism; a water bath was part of the rite of initiation when a Gentile converted to Judaism. Among the Essenes living at Qumran (home of the Dead Sea scrolls), ritual washings were very much a part of the community liturgy. We can conclude that the apostolic Church in its use of immersion in water to initiate converts into new life in Christ was adopting the meaningful cultic activity of its environment.

The New Testament community clearly understood that the coming of the Holy Spirit was connected with baptism. In Matthew 3, 11 and Luke 3, 16, John the Baptist compares his baptism with the baptism given by Jesus in the "Holy Spirit and fire." There is a relationship between Jesus' baptism in the Jordan and later Christian baptism. "He on whom you see the Spirit descend and remain, this is he who baptizes with the Holy Spirit" (Jn. 1, 33). While John's baptism led to Christian baptism, it did not have the same quality or significance. It was the descent of the Holy Spirit which turned a purification rite into a sacrament of the Holy Spirit's coming. John's rite received new meaning as soon as the first Christians experienced the coming of the Holy Spirit on Pentecost.

In John 3, 1-21 we have the story of Jesus' conversation with Nicodemus. Here is one of the few New Testament passages where Jesus himself speaks of baptism. Verses 2 to 8 indicate that being born from on high through the Spirit is necessary for entrance into the kingdom of God; natural birth is insufficient. In the text, the early Christians saw the close connection between baptism and the Holy Spirit: ". . . I say to you, unless one is born of water and the Spirit he cannot enter the kingdom of God" (Jn. 3, 5).

In the Acts of the Apostles there are five accounts which relate the Spirit to baptism in the name of Jesus: the story of Pentecost (Acts 2) which we have already examined, Philip baptizing the Samaritan (Acts 8), Paul's baptism by Ananias (Acts 9, 18f.), the baptism of Cornelius (Acts 10), and the baptism of the disciples at Ephesus (Acts 19). All these incidents tell us that the Spirit has a close if not inseparable connection with baptism as practiced in Acts.

The text in Acts 8 is a bit difficult. Although a number of Samaritans had believed and been baptized, Luke tells us that Peter and John had to come down from the mother Church "to pray for them that they might receive the Holy Spirit; for it had not yet fallen on any of them, but they had only been baptized in the name of the Lord Jesus. Then they laid their hands on them and they received the Holy Spirit" (Acts 8, 15-17). Scholars have various interpretations of this text. It may indicate the need of a further ministry than Philip's for the fullness of Christian initiation. Or it may indicate the desire of the home Church to approve and confirm the evangelization of its missionaries. At any rate two things are clear: (1) those baptized in the name of Jesus ought to be filled with the Holy Spirit; (2) after the apostles laid hands on the converts, the presence of the Spirit was concretely manifest, for Simon the Magician wanted to share the power of bestowing the Holy Spirit.

The connection between baptism and being filled with the Holy Spirit is evidenced in Acts 9 where Paul is baptized and receives the Holy Spirit through the ministry of Ananias, who was not one of the apostles. "So Ananias departed and entered the house. And laying his hands on him, he said: 'Brother Saul, the Lord Jesus who appeared to you on the road by which you came, has sent me that you may regain your sight and be filled with the Holy Spirit.' And immediately something like scales fell from his eyes and he regained his sight. Then he rose and was baptized and took food and was strengthened" (Acts 9, 17-19). As we have seen before, the consequence of Paul's baptism, his infilling with the Holy Spirit and his healing is that he began the office of proclaiming the Gospel (Acts 9, 20).

The situation is somewhat different in Acts 10 which recounts the initiation of the Roman centurion Cornelius and his household. The text is important in regard to the early Church's growing awareness that the Gospel was to be preached to all men. In this account Peter and Cornelius have been led together by the Lord. Cornelius asks Peter to tell them all that he had been taught by the Lord. In verses 34-43 Peter preaches a sermon containing a simple proclamation of the good news of salvation in Christ. "While Peter was still saying this the Holy Spirit fell on all who heard the word. And the believers from among the circumcised who came with Peter were amazed because the gift of the Holy Spirit had been poured out even on the Gentiles. For they heard them speaking in tongues and extolling God. Then Peter declared, 'Can anyone forbid water for baptizing these people who have received the Holy Spirit just as we have?' And he commanded them to be baptized in the name of Jesus Christ" (Acts 10, 44-48).

As in Acts 8 the water bath demanded the outpouring of the Spirit upon the Samaritans, here the outpouring of the Spirit demands baptism with water. Water and Spirit remain closely bound together. Note, too, that the manifestation of the Holy Spirit having fallen on them was their "speaking in tongues and extolling God."

Finally we will look at the baptism of the disciples in Ephesus found in Acts 19, 1-7. "While Apollos was at Corinth, Paul passed through the upper country and came to Ephesus. There he found some disciples. And he said to them, 'Did you receive the Holy Spirit when you believed?' And they said, 'No, we have never even heard that there is a Holy Spirit." And he said, 'Into what then were you baptized?' They said, 'Into John's baptism.' And Paul said, 'John baptized with the baptism of repentence telling the people to believe in the one who was to come after him, that is, Jesus.' On hearing this, they were baptized in the name of the Lord Jesus. And when Paul had laid his hands upon them, the Holy Spirit came on them; and they spoke with tongues and prophesied."

Paul senses that there is something wrong with the initiation of this group of disciples. He tests them by asking if they have been baptized in the Holy Spirit. Discovering their need for Christian initiation, he baptizes them and lays hands on them that they might receive the Holy Spirit. Once again the infilling of the Spirit is attested by the initiates entering upon the activities of speaking in tongues and prophesying.

What can be concluded from these episodes in Acts? They all make direct reference to the Spirit in connection with baptism. The Pentecost outpouring, the wellspring of Christian baptism, is a baptism in the Spirit, and at least in these instances the Spirit is always received in the baptismal context in some way. Thus the baptismal event, the liturgical celebration of conversion and initiation into the death and resurrection of Christ is the normal and basic setting for the imparting of the Holy Spirit. It can be said that to join the believers, to come alive in Christ, meant to receive the Holy Spirit and thus begin the Christian life. The beginning of the life in the Spirit, according to these texts, is always marked in some manifest way: speaking in tongues, prophesying, healing—which are not only signs of the presence of the Spirit but also gifts of the Spirit (1 Cor. 12) that play a functional role in the effective preaching of the Gospel by the newly initiated Christians.

There is one more question to be taken up before we have the full picture of how converts to Christ

received the Holy Spirit in the New Testament record,
that is: What is the role of the laying on of hands in
this process? Just as the water bath was taken by the
Church from common religious experience and given
a new meaning and effect, so also was the practice
of laying on hands. In the Old Testament the rite
was used with (1) the offering of sacrifice (Lev. 1,
3f.), (2) the consecration of Levites (Num. 8, 10),
and (3) the imparting of a blessing (Gen. 48, 14).
In the New Testament this gesture is used in connection with healing (cf. Mk. 5, 23; 7, 32; 8, 23-25; Acts
9, 12-17; 28, 8); (2) baptizing (cf. Acts 8, 17-19; 19, 5f.
and perhaps Heb. 6, 2); and (3) the distribution of
functions or offices in the Church (Acts 6, 6; 13, 3;
1 Tim. 4, 14; 2 Tim. 1, 6). As a ritual gesture then it
can have different purposes in different situations.
In connection with the baptism in the Holy Spirit it
seems to have been employed, at least sometimes, in
the apostolic Church in the context of baptismal
initiation. It does not seem in this regard to be a rite
independent of baptism. It is used with or to complete
the baptismal process, e.g., Peter and John in Samaria,
or Ananias with Paul. But it is not necessary for the
reception of the Spirit, e.g., Cornelius, or Pentecost
day itself. It may be part of, but is secondary to,
incorporation into the Body of Christ through the
bath of regeneration.

In conclusion, we need to return to this thought:
The Spirit dwells in and enlivens the community of
believers. To be filled with the Holy Spirit in the
New Testament Church meant basically to be fully
initiated into the community. Throughout Acts and
the epistles there are continual references to Christian
life and activity being in, of, and by the Holy Spirit.

The New Testament writers are extremely conscious that life in Christ means life in the Spirit, that the apostolate of the Church was the work of the Spirit, that an individual Christian vocation or office was a gift of the Spirit. To receive the Holy Spirit or to be filled with the Holy Spirit was not one event which was over and done with. Rather it was to enter upon the fullness of life in Christ, and as a member of his body to go about the task of drawing all things to completion in him. Pentecost, as the realization of the resurrection in the earthly Body of Christ, is an ongoing and growing reality by which the Kingdom is established and prepared for the return of the Lord in glory.

The Baptism in the Holy Spirit in the Patristic Church

In our consideration of the continued outpouring of the Holy Spirit on the Church in and through the Church, we will leave behind the testimony of the word and turn to the history and practice of the Church. As the Gospel spread across the Roman Empire, as communities of Christians grew up and became established in the cities of the East, North Africa, and Europe, through what forms of ecclesial celebration did the "baptism of the Holy Spirit and fire" take place?

It would seem that the baptism that Jesus gives—baptism in the Spirit—came to be identified with the Christian sacraments of initiation. When we talk about sacraments we are talking about a bestowal of grace in and through a visibly manifest form. Put more simply, God, having created man as a corporeal sentient person, approaches man in the power of his

Spirit through concrete, perceptible signs or instruments like water or the gesture of laying on hands. These corporeal realities—words, rites, gestures—are the actions of the Spirit-filled Body of Christ, they are instruments through which the Spirit approaches man and man responds. On the deep human level of religious celebration they perpetuate and communicate in space and time the paschal mystery of Christ.

As the community of believers developed into a clear-cut society in the world, its liturgical celebration rooted in the New Testament Church, blossomed forth in a beautiful employment of rites, gestures, and symbols natural to human religion. The reality of salvation and the outpouring of the Spirit are continued through these forms.

The sacraments of initiation, which are basically the direct continuation of the New Testament baptism and outpouring of the Spirit, developed into a rich liturgy during the first few centuries of the Church's history. While it is not to our purpose to give a detailed analysis of this liturgy, a brief examination of it will help us to understand later developments in sacramental practice.

In the early Church, as can be seen so clearly in St. Paul's letters, to be baptized was to enter the community of faith and the life of the Spirit by dying and rising with Christ. Initiation was incorporation into Christ's paschal mystery. It is not surprising then that Christian initiation was normally celebrated on that one special night in the whole year in which the paschal mystery was most fully recalled and celebrated—the Easter vigil. Within a relatively short time, when there were large numbers of converts in a city or district, initiation was also held on the vigil of Pentecost.

The candidates who presented themselves for baptism on those nights had been through a period of catechumenate lasting from seven weeks to two years, depending on local custom. Although there are significant variations in the rite from place to place, in the third, fourth and fifth centuries the following basic rite was practiced in both East and West:

(1) After some preliminaries, the assembled candidates were immersed three times in a water bath in the name of the Trinity.

(2) They were anointed all over with oil.

(3) They received a laying on of hands and/or a signing on the forehead.

(4) They celebrated and received the eucharist for the first time with the whole congregation.

The first and most important thing to be noticed about this rite of initiation is that it was conceived and celebrated as a totality. Within the context of the great annual celebration of the death and resurrection of Jesus, new brothers and sisters in Christ were born into the Body through the bath of regeneration and reception of the Holy Spirit. They were brought immediately to the table of the Lord, to enter upon the fully mature activity of the Spirit-filled People of God, the proclamation of the death and resurrection of Jesus in anticipation of his second coming. This one sweeping movement from baptistry to altar was not thought of in terms of separate sacraments but rather as one all encompassing action, often called simply "the sacrament" or "the mystery." Very often the whole process was termed "baptism" by the authors of that day. What is clear is that we have one event within which occurs simultaneously, if not indistinguishably, regeneration and the outpouring of the Spirit. The two are as closely related as they were in the New Testament Church.

While we set forth four basic actions within one event, it is true that there was considerable local variation in the rites. There was always a water bath. It might have been preceded by exorcisms and anointings. Sometimes while there was an anointing before the bath there was none after it. There was usually a laying on of hands after the bath and anointing, although in some places the imposition of hands was simultaneous with the triple immersion. The laying on of hands may have been done either by one of the presbyters or by the bishop of the local congregation. In some sources the imposition of hands is not clear, and in its place we find a signing with chrism by the bishop on the candidate's forehead, and maybe also on the mouth, nose, breast, and on the other senses. One may rightly ask how and why the use of oil developed. Anointing with oil, usually from head to foot, after taking a bath was part of the normal hygienic practice of the ancient world. The practice continued with the sacred bath and soon was given a mystical significance. On one point there is no variation: the rite always and everywhere concluded with the communal celebration of the eucharist, the sacrificial meal of the Mystical Body of Christ. This whole rite in the Church of the first five centuries was the baptism in the Holy Spirit.

It is interesting to discover what the Fathers of the Church said about the various parts of the rites of initiation, particulary in regard to the outpouring of the Spirit. Several points are universally agreed upon:

(1) The Holy Spirit is operative in the whole rite, working in and through the sacramental signs.

(2) The neophyte is born again in the rite; he puts off the old man, is plunged into the death and resurrection of Christ, and comes up a new man in Christ.

(3) The neophyte receives the Holy Spirit in the process together with the gifts and fruits of the Spirit.

But once again we find myriad interpretations of the various parts of the rite. For some the Holy Spirit was poured out in the bath just as the Spirit descended on Jesus in the Jordan. Other Fathers associated the imparting of the Spirit with the anointing with oil. The majority saw a double significance in the anointing. On one hand through the sign of oil we are anointed with the Holy Spirit, and at the same time by the Spirit we are conformed to Christ, for the word "Christ" means The Anointed, thus anointing is literally christening. It seems that the majority of the Fathers connected the outpouring of the Spirit with the anointing. But it must be remembered that the anointing took place only in conjunction with the bath. Still others, while seeing an outpouring of the Spirit in the bath-anointing believed the outpouring was made explicit and operative in the laying on of hands. Again this depended on local custom and emphasis. In those Churches where the imposition of hands was done not by just any presbyter but by the bishop of the church, it carried the force of confirming (not so much in the sense of imparting the Spirit, but in the sense of sealing, finishing, approving what had gone on at the font and formally recognizing or affiliating the neophyte with his Church). Finally there are a few writers who connected the outpouring of the Spirit with the first eucharistic meal itself.

What can we conclude from all of this? Basically we can say that Christian initiation was in the patristic Church one sacrament, generally called baptism, and that in the context of that one event both rebirth and the reception of the Holy Spirit took place. A reading of the texts of the rites and the baptismal catecheses which we possess indicates clearly that the fruits of the Spirit were an expected consequence of the rite, being characteristics of the life of the new man. The gifts of the Spirit were also expected. It is obvious that the Spirit gave one a ministry and function in the community, a share in the priesthood of Christ for the celebration of the eucharist, and that other Spirit-given offices were implicit and could be called forth on the basis of this baptismal outpouring. These offices included deaconess, exorcist, catechist, presbyter, or bishop. When the texts speak of the gifts of the Spirit they are enumerated according to the list in Isaiah rather than in 1 Cor. 12. This poses questions of greater interest about charismatic expectation in the Church, to which we shall return presently. The only important point here is that in the early centuries, to be filled with the Spirit, to receive the gifts and fruits of the Spirit for life in Christ was a thoroughly integrated part of the paschal and pentecostal baptismal rites.

The Charismatic Life in the Patristic Church

We face a serious problem on the question of

charismatic expectation in the patristic rites of initiation. In the New Testament, being filled with the Spirit resulted in ministries of healing, prophecy, discernment, and speaking in tongues. Why don't we hear of these gifts of the Spirit in connection with Christian baptism in the patristic era? This puzzling question has never been satisfactorily answered. Some considerations have been suggested in the past. All of them need investigation.

(1) All the offices of the Church, all the stations in the Church from bishop to simple baptized believer, were considered the work and appointment of the Holy Spirit. These gifts were thought of as charismatic.

(2) However the offices within the Church by the patristic era were becoming increasingly institutionalized, organized and controlled. While properly thought of as the work of the Spirit, the intervention and guidance of the Spirit seemed more remote.

(3) The Church as a whole was becoming socially acceptable and eventually established in the empire. An inevitable result of this was the further institutionalization of the Church along imperial lines and the entrance of local politics and factionalism into the government of the Church. This could have led to a lack of openness in the Church to the gifts of the Spirit, in fact given but not received.

(4) On the other hand, it can be asked if the New Testament charismatic activity had a peculiarly eschatological significance, being tools for proclaiming the Gospel in a crisis time of establishing the Kingdom. As the Church settled down to a more incarnational program, was the need for such striking

charismata less strongly felt, with a consequent decrease in their experience?

(5) Did the Church as a whole shy away from some of the gifts of the Spirit in strong reaction to those charismatic movements within it which emphasized tongues, visions and prophecy to the denial of the gifts of authority, judgment and government?

(6) We must realize that while the initiation rites may not speak directly of Paul's gifts of the Spirit, these charismata were in fact evidently experienced in many parts of the Church. The many stories of visions, dreams, prophecies, discernment, and healing, whether taking place in Augustine's city parish in Hippo or among the Fathers of the desert where the charismata abounded, cannot have arisen without some historical justification. The New Testament gifts did in fact continue in the Spirit-filled Church in the patristic, medieval and modern periods, although not at all times and in all places.

These considerations may indicate the cause of whatever decrease in charismatic activity occurred and the fact that the gifts of the Spirit, including the more dramatic, were not altogether absent from the life of the Church.

An Overview of Developments Since the Patristic Era

In a work of this type we make no pretension of adequately detailing the whole of Church history. That would be absurd. Yet a quick survey here may fill in a few large gaps in the intervening history.

Much scholarly work has been done, and much more needs to be done, in this particular area. It seems safe to say, however, that the eventual conversion of the Roman Empire and of the tribes of northern and western Europe brought about a radical disintegration of a unified liturgy of initiation. Huge dioceses, and too few bishops, priests, and catechists put a heavy strain on the established order. As kings and chieftains embraced Christianity, often from political and economic motives as well as from personal conversion, their peoples followed *en masse*. Adequate instruction was all too rare. Church historians seem sure that vast numbers of persons were baptized indiscriminately, without understanding what they were doing or the demands of a life turned to Jesus.

Because of the patterns of missionary journeys, baptism was separated from its two or three set times a year and was administered whenever possible. Throughout the sixth, seventh, and eighth centuries, and even up to the eleventh century in some areas of western Europe, baptism by a presbyter was regularly followed by his imposition of hands on the new Christian and the reception of first eucharist. In these cases the integrity of the rite was preserved. At the same time, from the sixth century onward as the Roman liturgy and law extended over Gaul, the British Isles, and finally Spain, the imposition of hands was separated from the baptismal rite and reserved to the local bishop, when and if he could get around to all his churches and missions. In this way a new rite called confirmation emerged as a separate sacrament. It was believed to have the role of imparting the Holy Spirit. This of course made considerable sense in the context of the whole baptismal liturgy, but because of poor education and a lack of historical perspective, the churchmen of the middle ages soon lost the knowledge of the integral

connection between the water bath and the laying
on of hands. Confirmation came to be regarded as a
second outpouring of the Holy Spirit. Theologians
were hard put to understand how one received the
Holy Spirit in baptism and again in confirmation.
In the Middle Ages a number of theologies of confirmation appeared in terms of the reception of the
strength to fight the Christian fight, or to preach the
Gospel in a life of witness, neither of which had
anything to do with the original rite. Even worse
explanations arose making confirmation a type of
Christian knighthood or an induction into Christ's
army.

It was not so much the theology of confirmation
that suffered but the practice of the sacrament itself.
To understand this one must realize that with the
exception of a few universities and monastic centers,
Europe was plunged into terrible ignorance. Often the
truths of the faith were neither well preached nor
understood, bishops and priests were poorly educated
and often illiterate. The lay folk were more spectators
at Mass than active participants and had as their
main source of Christian knowledge the often un-
reliable traditions of folklore.

We are quite sure that many, many of the Christian people never received confirmation. The people
seem never to have understood the need for it. While
they would go to any lengths to receive baptism, they
had little desire for confirmation. Secondly many
bishops were not too concerned about it, or they
simply could not reach all their flock. We have historical records which indicate that for long periods
of time in a number of places the bishops forgot to
confirm, either because they didn't understand it

themselves or because they didn't know of its practice.

In the cities and towns of later medieval Europe the practice of confirmation began to thrive again. But after passing through such a crisis, its precise relationship to the rest of the sacramental system and its meaning for Christian life were considerably weakened.

Since the sixteenth century the separate sacrament of confirmation has been regularly administered in the West in the Catholic Church. The text speaks of a sacramental outpouring of the Holy Spirit. In essence the text is taken from the appropriate sections of the ancient baptismal liturgy. Yet the theological problem remains: In what sense is this reception of the Spirit different from that in baptism? Popular catecheses about becoming a soldier of Christ or receiving the grace for a mature Christian life can be dismissed since it is clear that the source of mature life in Christ is preeminently the participation in the eucharist. Confirmation, once part of the organic process of Christian initiation into the eucharist, now stands apart and is received generally after first holy communion; it has, unfortunately, the look of a dangling participle.

The Church is acutely aware of the problem of the meaning and practice of confirmation. In its *Constitution on the Sacred Liturgy,* the Second Vatican Council directed its reform: "The rite of confirmation is to be revised and the intimate connection which this sacrament has with the whole of Christian initiation is to be more lucidly set forth; for this reason it will be fitting for candidates to renew their baptismal promises just before they are confirmed" (n. 71).

There is considerable controversy among Catholic liturgists as to how confirmation should be reformed. One party seeks the restoration of the rite' as part of the baptismal liturgy, to be administered by the ordinary minister of baptism. This would hold whether the person to be baptized is an infant or an adult. Another group (among whom are found advocates of adult baptism as the normal practice) hopes that confirmation will be the sacrament of young adulthood through which the confirmand will ratify of his own accord the baptismal initiation of his infancy.

It is not possible at this time to know which way the reform of confirmation will go. Indeed, the catechumenate and the practice of baptism are also undergoing serious scrutiny in terms of reform. But what we have seen in this brief historical survey should assure us that what is essentially meant by Jesus baptizing in the Holy Spirit should not be equated with the present rite of confirmation. In fact we can be more sure about what it means to be baptized in the Holy Spirit than about what it means to be confirmed.

4

Pentecostal Experience Today

At the private gatherings, a growing number of Catholics have been experiencing the same "baptism in the Spirit" that Protestant pentecostals experience.

The National Catholic Reporter

If the previous chapter has a major point to stress, it is this: most truly, most really, the baptism in the Holy Spirit is essentially a part of our Christian initiation, the sacrament of baptism and its ongoing actualization in our celebration of the eucharist and living the Christian life. What purpose then is there, one might ask, in a Catholic pentecostal movement seeking a baptism in the Holy Spirit with the gifts and fruits of the Holy Spirit? The answer lies in the fact that baptism in the Holy Spirit, as we use the term, has been poured out in the Church since Pentecost Sunday and through every complete baptismal celebration still today. The Church is filled with the Holy Spirit; as the Body of Christ, it has already received all the gifts and fruits of the Spirit. What this new pentecostal movement seeks to do through faithful prayer, and by trusting in the Word of God, is to ask the Lord to actualize in a concrete living way what the Christian people have already received. It is an attempt to respond in radical faith to the Spirit who has already been given so that his life, his gifts, and his fruit may be actualized in the lives of the members of Christ's Body.

To evangelical pentecostals, baptism in the Holy Spirit is a "new" work of grace. In the life of a Catholic it is an "old" work, yet practically "new" because the phrase as used by Catholic pentecostals is a prayer of renewal for everything that Christian initiation is and is meant to be. In practice it has come to be an experience of reaffirmation rather than of initiation. Among Catholic pentecostals this baptism is neither a new sacrament nor a substitute sacrament. Like the renewal of baptismal promises, it is a renewal in faith of the desire to be everything that Christ wants us to be. The phrase "baptism in the Holy Spirit" has been borrowed from fundamentalist pentecostals who don't have the sacramental theology needed to relate it to the whole context of water baptism. In the last seventy years it has acquired the sense given it by those who first encountered it in modern times: a definite experience of the person and work of the Holy Spirit in the life of the Church, followed by manifestations of the presence of the Spirit as detailed in the New Testament. For Catholics this experience is a renewal, making our initiation as children concrete and explicit on a mature level. It is in this sense that we speak of receiving the baptism in the Holy Spirit, in this chapter and throughout the book.

The men and women, clerics and lay people who have sought and received the baptism in the Holy Spirit are by and large ordinary Catholic people from every walk of life, profession and socio-economic bracket. They have shared the desire to be good Catholics and to grow in the life and love of Christ. Serious about their religion, concerned for the spiritual welfare of others, anxious for constructive renewal in the Church, they have been equally involved in their civic communities and employment, entering fully into all the normal activities which mark this period of our national life—human rights, law, justice, good government, peace. They have come to the baptism in the Spirit representing traditional and progressive trends in contemporary Catholicism. They have come from the opposing poles of right-wing Republicans and left-wing Democrats. They seem to be a healthy cross section of American Catholicism. But they have been united in one Lord, one faith, and one baptism by the desire to be more fully the type of Christian that Jesus wants them to be. They share, for all their differences of opinion, the belief that the Lord knows best what's right and needed in his Church. As a group they have the characteristics of serious Christian dedication, openness to the will of God, and the willingness to yield to him.

Yet this is not the complete picture, for there have been a number of people who have come face-to-face with the pentecostal movement as persons with minimal faith, or lost faith, or nominal Christian observance. These people have been touched by the witness of a friend or by a charismatic prayer group, and being attracted by it they have found for the first time real faith in Jesus Christ and the richness of life in the Spirit.

To renew their baptismal commitment, to live concretely in the Spirit of Christ, hundreds of American Catholics have prayed to be baptized in the Holy

Spirit. There is no set form or formula or setting for this type of prayer. It takes place in small or large prayer groups, with a friend or alone—but always with Jesus. It takes place with the laying on of hands or without this gesture, at home, at school, at work, at Mass, in the car—but always in expectant faith.

In fact if there is any one thing which most strikingly characterizes Catholic pentecostals it is not tongues or singing or prayer groups; it is that they came to seek a renewal in the Holy Spirit in simple faith, and having received the answer to their prayer they begin to walk in a newness of faith. The people involved in the charismatic renewal are basically men and women of new, richer faith.

Faith, of course, is a gift of God, a grace, an unearned favor. It comes to one, in the plan of redemption, by hearing and believing the word of God, by witnessing the life of the word lived out in the lives of Christians, by seeing the results of faith in the beauty of those around us. The life of witness is the life of the Church, it is the lived out proclamation of the good news of salvation. Through preaching in action, the Spirit draws men to God in Christ and the life of faith is born.

When men of faith pray with expectation, Christ's answer builds up their faith. A man may come to seek baptism in the Holy Spirit because he has seen and believed the work of the Spirit in the life of a friend. He then trusts Jesus in prayer and expects that the Lord will renew in him the gifts and fruits bestowed in baptism but not fully actualized in a living way. In the answer to that prayer, Jesus often becomes more real to the believer. He is much closer, more present and active in one's life. He is not only enthroned at the "right hand of the Father," but he, the risen Lord, is also really alive among the members of his body. This old belief becomes a new awareness, becomes really real to the believers. The relationship of faith between this man and the Father through Christ has been deepened, transformed, and has become the center of personal existence. It would be false to characterize this new found faith-life as a purely emotional experience. Certainly human emotion is involved in any act of love, and people respond emotionally according to their temperament. But it seems better to speak of this new faith life on the level of a penetrating and all-encompassing awareness and conviction which involves the whole body-person, with all his human qualities in a response of deep commitment.

It may be asked if this subjective trusting faith which radically believes in the present action of the Lord is justified. Isn't it somewhat presumptuous? Doesn't it tend to tell Jesus what he should be about? Not really. After all, faith like anything else, should be judged by its fruits. An evaluation of this new faith-life shows an increase in the fruits of the Spirit and the authentic growth of personal and communal spiritual life. The evidence in the lives of other Christians to this prayer in radical faith should be justification enough.

Secondly, it does not seem presumptuous to pray for the actualization of what we know Jesus has promised to and bestowed upon his Church—that is, the counsel, teaching, life, and power of his Spirit. To pray for such realities is simply to take Jesus at his word and accept what is already there.

Thirdly, there is an authoritative basis **for this**

type of prayer in faith of the word of God. It is important to study and understand the implications of the following statements of Jesus for the life of the Church.

"And I tell you, ask, and it will be given to you; seek and you will find; knock, and it will be opened to you. For everyone who asks receives, and he who seeks finds, and to him who knocks it will be opened . . . If you then who are evil know how to give good gifts to your children, how much more will the heavenly Father give the Holy Spirit to those who ask him" (Lk. 11, 9-13).

"Therefore I tell you, whatever you ask in prayer, believe that you receive it, and you will" (Mk. 11, 24).

"For truly I say to you if you have faith as a grain of mustard seed, you will say to this mountain, 'Move hence to yonder place,' and it will move; and nothing will be impossible to you" (Mt. 17, 20).

"And whatever you ask in prayer you will receive, if you have faith" (Mt. 21, 22).

"If you abide in me, and my words abide in you, ask whatever you will, and it shall be done for you" (Jn. 15, 7).

A few remarks on these texts:

(1) We must be careful not to take these texts out of context, and the passages in which they appear should be studied to catch their full force.

(2) We should be aware that hyperbolic speech is often found in the New Testament.

(3) The texts, however, are dominical sayings, that is, words which the New Testament community recalls in faith to be the words and/or the mind of the Lord for the Church.

(4) Their collective force reiterates the basic

call of Jesus that his disciples believe in him. Therefore they say something very basic and fundamental about the attitude of faith and confidence Jesus expects his followers to share when they pray.

(5) In such an attitude of faith, authentic prayer is still seeking first of all the will of God (1 Jn. 5, 14-15). This applies preeminently to the outpouring of the Holy Spirit in the Church which we know to be the will of Jesus from his word.

The prayer of faith for a renewal of the work in the Holy Spirit is not presumptuous or demanding; it is simply an acceptance by faith and by experience of what Jesus has done for his body and an opening of ourselves to respond fully to his will.

If anything has been renewed, enlivened or rediscovered by Catholics in the pentecostal movement it has been this new emphasis on a life of radical faith in the loving presence of the risen Lord in our midst by the power of his Spirit. This renewal of faith, rising up among us in such close connection with the Year of Faith, seems destined to play an even greater role as it suffuses and enlivens the several movements of renewal within the Church: liturgical and scriptural, reform of clerical and religious life, the ascendency of the laity to full responsibility as the People of God, and in the broad field of ecumenical relationships. We can also expect the effect of this lively faith in Christian involvement in the vital crises of political, social, and economic development in the world.

Prayer for baptism in the Holy Spirit is, most simply, a prayer in expectant faith that an individual's or community's baptismal initiation be existentially renewed and actualized. More on this subject will be said later, but as we already noted, our experience

indicates that the Lord Jesus accomplishes the renewal in each individual in many different situations
through no specific form. Only one thing seems to be
essential: an authentic request, radical, open and
available to the answer that the Lord *will* send.

Many persons have received the baptism in the
Holy Spirit in private, when, alone and in prayer,
they are flooded with the peace and joy of Christ.
Frequently they begin praising God in a new language. The majority of persons have experienced this
renewal in a prayer group or while praying with at
least one other person. This makes a great deal of
sense in light of the communal nature of Christian
life and the current rediscovery or emphasis placed
upon the mutual help and service characteristic of the
relationships among members of the one Body of
Christ. This group prayer and ministry is often
referred to as "praying with someone for the baptism
in the Holy Spirit." We are reminded of such sayings
of Jesus as: "If two of you agree on earth about
anything they ask, it will be done for them by my
Father in heaven. For where two or three are gathered
in my name, there am I in the midst of them" (Mt.
18, 19-20). The baptism in the Spirit is most often a
community celebration of the ongoing reality of
Pentecost in the Church.

Group prayer is often accompanied by an imposition of hands on the head or shoulders of the one the
group is praying for. Yet this does not always happen;
many people receive baptism in the Holy Spirit without the laying on of hands. While it may not be
necessary, Catholic pentecostals are hardly indifferent
about it. The value of this gesture is unanimously

attested; for with and through it the Lord often makes real the renewal of his Spirit.

For Protestant pentecostals who have little developed sacramental theology, the adaptation of the laying on of hands was a daring step in 1901. They did it in simple imitation of the New Testament scenes which depicted an outpouring of the Spirit. They saw it as an instrument used by God for this purpose among others.

We have already seen that this gesture has many uses in scripture. In the New Testament it can be part of a baptismal initiation, or the bestowal of an office within the community, or in praying for the sick. Throughout the history of the Church the laying on of hands has had many uses both within the sacramental rites (initiation, ordination) and in the extra-sacramental prayer life of the people. Catechists often laid hands on their pupils after class. Priests place their hands on the heads of people they bless. In some countries fathers lay hands on their children while blessing them at night, and superiors of religious houses have a similar custom.

The use of the laying on of hands by pentecostal groups now comes into perspective. Although not necessary, it is a common practice because:

(1) It is a spontaneous religious gesture found in religions throughout the world.

(2) It is a sign of mutual concern and solidarity; it binds together in a symbolic way those praying, at the same time indicating the one for whom they are praying.

(3) It is a prayer in action; a corporeal manifestation and embodiment of prayer, which makes the prayer more concrete, clearly a "here and now" event.

Man needs such physical things in his encounters with the transcendent God.

(4) Experience has proved it helpful in renewing the life of the Spirit and inaugurating a deeper faith-life full of the gifts and fruits of the Spirit.

Catholic pentecostals may think of this form of the baptism in the Holy Spirit as sacramental in the broad sense of the term—that is, as all physical realities speak to us of the grace of God. But the baptism in the Spirit, as pointed out above, is not thought of as one of the specific sacramental celebrations which are liturgical acts of the Church in extension of Christ's paschal mystery. It should be clear that the baptism in the Holy Spirit is not a sacrament nor a replacement for any sacrament. Far from it. For without the sacramental life of the Church as its basis, the prayer for a renewal in the Holy Spirit would be meaningless. The baptism in the Holy Spirit, as the term is commonly used by Catholic pentecostals, is precisely a prayer for the renewal and actualization of baptismal initiation. It is, if such a radical distinction needs to be made, a prayer not a sacrament.

Nor are pentecostal prayer groups imparting the Holy Spirit. There is only one person who imparts the Holy Spirit, the risen Lord Jesus who continually pours out his Spirit on the Church. He is the one who baptizes in the Holy Spirit. Thus the sacrament of baptism is most properly seen not only as the action of the Church, his Body, but also of himself personally. Through sacramental baptismal initiation, the imparting of the Spirit by Jesus is communicated in the context of community worship to a new member of Christ's Body. This is most basically the baptism in the Holy Spirit. What the charismatic prayer group is doing is praying in expectant faith for the concrete renewal and continuation of the baptism in the Spirit in the life of the person who wants to live fully in Christ. They are not imparting the Spirit, for the Spirit has already been given; but they are claiming in faith and according to the mind of Jesus the mature experience of the power of the Holy Spirit. If we were to be more precise we would not talk of receiving the baptism in the Spirit but of renewing the baptism in the Spirit. To the present date however, fundamentalist terminology has prevailed. On the other hand, many people like the word "receive" because it speaks of a concrete and conscious experience of a reality they had before only vaguely understood.

The personal testimonies throughout this book speak eloquently enough of the result of baptism in the Holy Spirit. Perhaps these results can be expressed categorically in the following way.

First, on the level of what we may call the interior life or the spiritual life (although not isolated or individualistic), there is the remarkable deepening or transformation of faith-life described above. From the new faith relationship with Jesus, both individuals and communities find themselves growing more deeply in the fruits of the Spirit: love, joy, peace, patience, kindness, goodness, faithfulness, gentleness, self-control (Gal. 5, 22-23). These characteristics of the life of Christ increase in growth and fruitfulness in the lives of the charismatic Christian. This subject will be treated more fully in the next chapter. Here we just want to point out the tremendous significance of such a work of the Spirit for the integration of the life within the Body of

Christ. The love of Christ, mutual forebearance and concern, the lack of strife and contention within the community are all results of baptism in the Holy Spirit. How else could men and women of such diverse backgrounds, opinions, and desires live together as one? Yet again and again we have seen that they can and do live in a "harmony of difference."

Secondly, on the communal level is experienced the operation of the ministry gifts of the Holy Spirit. In the next chapter we will discuss the scope and varieties of gifts of the Spirit. Some of them are listed by Saint Paul in 1 Cor. 12: the utterance of wisdom, the utterance of understanding, the discernment of spirits, healing, prophecy, interpretation of tongues and speaking in strange tongues. Numerous examples of these gifts in operation have already been presented and will be discussed more fully. Here let us say only that the gifts of the Holy Spirit are not bestowed on individuals as a reward for exemplary Christian life; they are in no sense earned; rather they are poured out among a group of believers for the sake of building up the Church and of facilitating the proclamation of the Gospel. They are simply tools of the Body of Christ. If there is healing among us, it is the risen Lord Jesus who is the healer working through the members of his Body. If there is prophecy, it is not that some man or woman is a great prophet, but that the Spirit of Jesus speaks in the assembly.

It is this new life of faith for the individual and the community, with the experience of the gifts and fruits of the Spirit building up the Church and manifesting Christ to the world, which is the result of renewing our baptism in the Holy Spirit.

Some persons might wonder about the value of the Catholic pentecostal movement, seeing that pentecostalism originated outside the Catholic Church and has in fact flourished in new denominational forms. This question can be answered on several levels. First it should be remembered that the Catholic movement was started by Catholics. It began not through any Protestant pentecostal proselytization but because some renewal-minded Catholics prayed to the Holy Spirit that they might become better Catholics. While a healthy ecumenical aspect has developed in the movement and has been tremendously fruitful, its origin for us Catholics was primarily Catholic. In the last two years we have received word from a number of Catholic persons and prayer groups who received baptism in the Holy Spirit in a totally Catholic context, yet quite apart from the specific outpouring of the Spirit recorded in this book.

Secondly, we know that the Catholic Church has no monopoly on the Holy Spirit. The Holy Spirit exists wherever Jesus is confessed as Lord, throughout the broad spectrum of Christian denominations. Vatican II is very clear on this point. "Moreover some, even very many, of the most significant elements or endowments which together go to build up and give life to the Church herself can exist outside the visible boundaries of the Catholic Church; the written word of God, the life of grace; faith, hope, and charity, along with other interior gifts of the Holy Spirit and visible elements . . . Nor should we forget that whatever is wrought by the grace of the Holy Spirit in the hearts of our separated brethren can contribute to our own edification. Whatever is truly Christian never conflicts with the genuine interests of the faith; indeed, it can always result in a more ample realization of the very mystery of Christ and the Church" (*Decree on Ecumenism,* nn. 3-4).

Thirdly, we must not confuse the Catholic pentecostal movement with denominational pentecostalism. In both we find at the heart of the movement essentially the same experience of the Holy Spirit. For Catholics the experience is an important element in the whole life of worship, sacramental celebration, rich dogmatic tradition and apostolic work. Pentecostal denominations were formed by Christians who received the baptism in the Holy Spirit within certain other fundamentalist denominations and who were forced out of their home churches because others would not accept their experiences as valid. Thus for many pentecostal denominations the baptism in the Holy Spirit and the experience of the gifts has been such a central focus as to tend to exclude other rich facets of Christian community life.

Fourthly, we must not confuse the baptism in the Holy Spirit with the cultural forms of religious expression common in pentecostal denominations. These churches are offshoots of American revivalism, which had a great effect in shaping our society. Often rural and frontier in their style, the nineteenth and twentieth century revivals were marked by bombastic preaching and loud emotional response, by spontaneous prayer in a loud and perhaps exhibitionist style, by camp meetings under tents and "being saved on the Sawdust Trail." With the revivals came a simplistic and individualistic Christian ethic. The righteous life is characterized by "clean living," therefore no smoking, drinking, dancing, makeup, theatre going or other amusements. While considerably tempered over the last several decades, the revivalistic culture continues to pervade denominational pentecostalism. It is perhaps the gift box in which the gift comes among those people—but it is not to be confused with the gift itself. In its own cultural setting and development, this religious style is quite beautiful, meaningful and relevant. But it is not essential to nor desirable for the baptism in the Holy Spirit, especially among people of far different religious backgrounds. Pentecostals are often called "Holy Rollers" and advocates of "the old time religion." The social, cultural and doctrinal patterns of both Holy Rollers and the "old time religion" existed long before modern pentecostalism.

One final question: Granting the seeming goodness of the movement, its bearing of good fruit and all that, why should it happen in today's Church, in sharp contrast to our experience in former generations? In today's whole movement of renewal, characterized by a drawing together of clergy and laity, by a mutual confession of past failings, by a desire to purify the Bride of Christ, there is an openness of the whole Church to everything Jesus would have it be. In such an atmosphere Jesus is able to break through the walls of human weakness with the result that the charismatic life of the Church grows once again, alongside the growth in liturgy, scripture, and role of the laity.

Today the Church and the world are both in a time of severe crises, of religious, political, and economic revolutions. The relevance of Christianity to the world is severely challenged on all sides. The past sins of Christian people are bearing bad fruit while waves of bitterness rise up from young people and young nations in reaction to the old order. In this situation, Jesus along with the life of the Spirit is renewing the dramatic charisms of the Spirit—not only to build up the Church but to call attention to and communicate the good news of salvation.

To the Catholic Church of today, in the throes of renewal, the Lord Jesus has sent his blessings in many wonderful ways while challenging it to fuller life in him. One of the things he is doing among his people is making them more aware of the reality and power of his Holy Spirit. He is leading thousands of Catholics to experience, perhaps for the first time, the fruits of the Spirit in their own lives and in their relationships with the Father and with all men. Also experienced today, with many other good things, are the ministry gifts of the Spirit common in the New Testament Church. This outpouring, where it is received, is renewing the People of God. It is received by prayer in expectant faith that the Lord will renew in us his baptism in the Holy Spirit.

5

The Gifts and Fruit
of the Spirit

Through the use of a symbolic gesture known as the "laying on of hands" they pray for the gifts of the Holy Spirit described in Saint Paul.

These gifts include charity, wisdom, faith, prophecy, healing, discernment of spirits, speaking in tongues and interpretation of tongues...

While tongues is said to be a common occurrence in the pentecostal community at Notre Dame, it is considered only as an aid to the fruits of the Holy Spirit. These are catalogued as love, joy, peace, patience, kindness, and generosity. And, in all fairness, it must be said that these virtues are more pronounced in the pentecostal community than is the ability to speak in tongues.

They were particularly evident at the second meeting I attended. This time we met in a cheerful family room at the home of a Notre Dame physics professor [Paul DeCelles] and his wife [Jeanne]. Though we were strangers, we were welcomed like old friends. Except for the fact that no one was drinking, it seemed like a cocktail party.

The National Catholic Reporter

Birthdays are great occasions for all of us, to be celebrated with parties, balloons and presents. For gift-giving, that symbolic, corporeal, token giving of oneself seems to be part of any joyful and fully human event. But no gift is meant to sit on a shelf, unopened, unwrapped, unused, unknown. At baptism we celebrate our new birth-day. On that day we entered into a loving relationship with the Father who gave us his greatest gift—new life in Christ. But there are other gifts the Lord holds out to us. They have already been given. Should we not fully accept them?

The gifts referred to here are given not only for our own enjoyment but are charisms, meant to be used for the building up of the Body of Christ into which we have been incorporated. Some of these charisms, these gifts, are listed in the New Testament. Saint Paul in several places lists examples of the charisms meant to be present in the believing community: prophecy, service, teaching, exhortation, generosity, leadership, mercy, apostleship, evangelism, the word of wisdom, the word of knowledge, faith, healing, miracles, discernment of spirits, speaking in tongues, and interpretation of tongues. The list as it reads is long. But in reality, the list is endless. All of these charisms, mentioned by Saint Paul, are but examples, "for instances," of the types of ministry gifts meant to be operative in the Church of Christ. The charisms that Paul mentions are by no means meant to be exclusive. In each age, in each community, in each life, the gifts which the Spirit pours out must be newly discovered and accepted.

Everything in the life of the Church is a gift of the Spirit. Every role, every office, is to flow from and be filled with the Spirit. No division, no breach, is possible between charismatic and hierarchical elements in the Church as some would suppose, since the role of the hierarchy is itself meant to be charismatic, a Spirit-given office. And as new structures

evolve in the Church they, too, are meant to be filled
with the Spirit of God.

In the past we have seen functions develop within
the body—charisms—which have indeed been recognized as Spirit-filled. The role of cantor in the
assembly and the development of monastic life are in
this category. Yet we must be open to recognize not
only new charismatic roles but also subtle changes in
the old ones. In the early Church the deacon's job
was to see that the widows had enough to eat, that
housing and clothing were adequate for the needs
of those in the community. Because he also assisted
at ceremonies, his function became more and more
structured within a liturgical framework. It doesn't
take much analogy to see who performs his original
function as community caseworker. Today, the
Catholic social worker, alive with the love and power
of Jesus, is exercising an authentic gift of the Spirit.

Rapid, revolutionary changes in our world have
opened the vistas of Christian ministry to the whole of
mankind. The prophet-protester is as unsettling to
the comfortable and the corrupt now as ever he was
in the days of Ezekiel. And surely in an age where the
"medium is the message," a charism must be seen in
the Christian journalist-editor who incarnates himself
radically in the midst of the communications media.
New needs in the body of Christ call for new ministries of the Spirit. How can we say that charisms are
not meant for the twentieth century and still maintain
that the Lord still is guiding his Church? Will the
risen Lord and Savior of all creation withdraw his
Spirit from all structures, from all people but those
of his historical century? We cannot believe this is so.

The Second Vatican Council remains the central

and most obvious sign-gift of the Spirit in our day. It literally shouts to us that "clearly the Spirit is guiding his people." Whole groups of Christians have been swept up by the Spirit to lead in renewal and reform movements. The liturgical, ecumenical, and scriptural movements stand foremost among these sovereign gifts of God. Each one speaks to some particular need, from one particular standpoint within the whole program of renewal. The liturgical movement speaks to God's people in terms of celebration, the ecumenical movement in terms of fellowship, and the scriptural revival from the perspective of communication of the living word. It is in this context of renewal and revival that the pentecostal movement (if such it may be termed) stands as a witness in terms of the here and now reality of the risen Lord in power. It is in this context of renewal and revival, that we would like to present the charismatic life as it seems to be presented—to us—today.

While it should be clear from all that was just said that we must be ever open and watchful of the splendid rainbow of gifts that the Spirit would show forth to us, we would like to return to the original list of charisms or gifts listed by Saint Paul as the focal point of our discussion. For it is to these charisms that we have been drawn in our concrete experience of renewal. The shattering difference that this "movement" of the Spirit among us has wrought, is an unexpected return to the primitive list of ministry gifts as mentioned in First Corinthians 12, 8-10. They are, the word of wisdom, of knowledge, faith, healing, miracles, prophecy, discernment of spirits, speaking in tongues and interpretation of tongues. Our highly differentiated and contemporary

Christian community is quite naturally shocked to confront the reality of these charisms today. But a rather crude expression from the ranks of the "hippies" will serve to express our understanding of this as perfectly as we can see it: everyone, every member within the Body of Christ has his "thing." Saint Paul, who we know had the gift of tongues and who exercised the gift of healing, was nonetheless preeminently an evangelist. To be an itinerant wanderer for the Lord, that was his "thing," his gift, his call. He fulfilled many functions within the Body of Christ—but one stands out as primary over all the others. Each of us has been called by God to use every gift he has given us in his service. We, like Paul must fulfull many functions and throw ourselves fully into the many tasks, concerns and involvements of the committed Christian life in our day. But, like Paul, we are also called to focus our charismatic service, to find our primary gift, our "thing."

We who have come to experience this "new Pentecost," this new outpouring of the Spirit with all the accompanying manifestations, are convinced that these ministry gifts are renewed here and now to play a specific role in the renewal of the Church in the world of today. We are not saying that only the gifts listed in First Corinthians are charisms. All other gifts of the Spirit in his Church are charismatic as well. But for us it is obvious that some of us are meant to bring these specific gifts, to the tasks, concerns, and involvements of Christian life today. They have come to be operative in the Christian community not as the totality of all gifts, nor to the exclusion of the simultaneous exercise of other gifts that go to build up the Body of Christ in the world, but as our preeminent call, focal point, witness and primary gift. It seems to be our "thing."

Attempts to categorize the nine gifts vary from author to author. Some divide them into two camps, gifts of utterance and gifts of power. Others subdivide them further into gifts of teaching, exhortation, confirmation, service, etc. We intend simply to describe each of the gifts as they are experienced and then to show them in the context of community worship in which they are to be most fully understood. Though each of these gifts is uniquely different, there is a close link, an interdependence in their exercise which is beautiful to see. We will watch for the interrelationship of gifts as well.

The Word of Wisdom

Foremost among the gifts which the Spirit bestows is wisdom. There is an attitude of childlike simplicity which opens us to these gifts. In entering into our new life, we often experience these realities like small children. Groping, searching, still in awe at the wonder of it all—it is no accident that the gift of tongues, that childlike babble, is therefore the first gift usually experienced. The other gifts of the Spirit, especially such an exalted one as wisdom, being less spectacular, we discover as we begin to toddle around. In fact very often we find we've been "playing with" it for some time but did not know its name. This is our experience with the word of wisdom. In the first few weeks and months of this pentecostal "outburst," one ability, one power seemed to be very evident in a few individuals. We came to call this (for want of a better name) the "gift of inspired preaching." That's what it was. But it was also the word of wisdom unrecognized as such. When one of these individuals stood before a group to proclaim the Good News of Christ, there was a piercing, penetrating quality to his words which struck the root, the core of every listener. We had heard the same words before; we had in many cases heard the same speaker before; but now into his proclamation came a new dynamism, a new conviction, a new penetration, which hushed and stirred us all.

Wisdom is not particularly exotic, alluring or exciting. As a spoken word it carries the peace, the will, and the authority of the Lord. It may be missed. In our stumbling way as we began to walk in the way of the Spirit, using these gifts, we began to refer to every gift of utterance as prophecy—which, of course, it was, using "prophecy" in the broadest sense of the term. For example we knew that when a problem arose in the community and an important decision had to be made, if we would gather to pray the Lord would speak through us to give light and direction. At one point amid the confusion and ramblings someone would speak forth, and immediately from that point onward there would be no need to seek further. We knew that without it being infallible the "supremely right thing" had just been said, and the task now became clear. All actions should carry out the plan that had been spoken. We have come to expect that gift to be operative when we meet for such important decisions. We got in the habit of praying during such meetings for a "prophecy" from the Lord for direction. When it came, we knew it. But what we now begin to see, is that when it came it was the "word of wisdom."

In Acts 6, 1-5, the apostles had a similar meeting

for a problem which had arisen in the community, and
we have an example of the word of wisdom operating.
"Now in those days as the number of the disciples
was increasing, there arose a murmuring among the
Hellenists against the Hebrews that their widows
were being neglected in the daily ministration. So
the Twelve called together the multitude of the
disciples and said, "It is not right that we should
give up preaching the word of God and serve tables.
Therefore, brethren, pick out from among you seven
men of good repute, full of the Spirit and of wisdom,
whom we may appoint to this duty. But we will devote
ourselves to prayer and to the ministry of the word.
And what they said pleased the whole multitude . . ."
That plan which meets the approval of the "whole
multitude," that penetrating word which shows
clearly what the Lord would have us do, that word
which cuts us to the heart with its truth and might—
that is the word of wisdom.

It is one gift which is obviously very closely related
to gifts of preaching, leadership and counsel in the
community. This wisdom we speak of is not an
abiding personal characteristic (the "naturally"
sagacious man). It is more than a permanent human
talent, yet it certainly is grounded in and thrives upon
a strong foundation of knowledge, prudence and
familiarity with the word of God. And it remains a
gift of utterance. It speaks a word to one moment
and to no other. When it is heard, "something happens." To all who have ears, "let them hear."

The Word of Knowledge

Interpreters vary in their attempts to determine
exactly what Saint Paul means by the various gifts of

the Spirit. This is especially true of "the word of knowledge." Our "probable" opinion comes from experience—where it seems to have both an individual and communal level of operation. In the former case it closely resembles the gift of discernment at first glance, but it is different in operation. Many times, for example, we would find ourselves with a stranger and after only minutes the knowledge of what they needed to hear would be on our lips. Suddenly, inexorably, we would see to the root of the need or the problem of a person. When spoken, this is indeed a word of knowledge, but since the gifts are given not only to individuals but to the Church, for the Church, it becomes obvious that the more frequent exercise of this gift will be ecclesial in nature. Its function is to speak the word of knowledge to all in the community here and now. It is no wonder then that we see a close connection between this gift and the gift of teaching. This is not to say that all teaching in the Church involves this gift. (Would that it did!) But once again this gift, when present, is known. It is recognized. We will recognize it as long as we are not looking for thunder and lightening. A gentle rain can water the parched earth as well as a cloudburst. If we are unable to see the manifestations of the Spirit unless they are spectacular, we may miss them altogether. Over and over again we have found in our gatherings that, as with the word of wisdom when the word of knowledge is spoken, the truths may be old, the speaker the same, and yet at that moment the lesson sinks in, penetrates, confounds and refreshes as never before. At that moment the quality, tone, presentation, and content is such that we can only describe it in the terminology of our evangelical brothers. It is "anointed." "When the Spirit of truth comes, he will guide you into all the truth" (Jn. 16, 13).

Faith

To respond, to listen, to accept the word of God initially is in itself a gift of God. The faith, the choice, the radical committment of ourselves to Jesus is a leap of love. Why then is faith listed as a consequence of our response and acceptance? Faith that says "yes" to Jesus initially need be only a quiet "amen" to the call of God. With that the Lord can work. But the faith that serves a charismatic function is quite different. It is the faith of Job, unshakable in the midst of adversity, of Abraham in the face of absurdity, of Peter setting his foot on the water. It is faith that dares to believe that God will be true to his Word no matter how impossible the situation.

Consider this example from Acts: "Now Peter and John were going up to the temple at the hour of prayer, the ninth hour. And a man lame from birth was being carried, whom they laid daily at the gate of the temple which is called Beautiful to ask alms of those who entered the temple. Seeing Peter and John about to go into the temple, he asked for alms. And Peter directed his gaze at him, with John, and said, 'Look at us.' And he fixed his attention upon them, expecting to receive something from them. But Peter said, 'I have no silver and gold, but I give you what I have; in the name of Jesus Christ of Nazareth, walk'" (Acts 3, 1-6).

What is important here is not the miracle, not the healing (for the beggar did arise and walk). What we should see here is the gift of faith that Peter had to have to be able to believe that God would heal

this man. It is easy to say "I believe God can heal."
It is quite another thing to say "I believe God can
heal right now—in this situation." That faith which
dares to believe the ultimate and to claim it is a gift
of the Spirit. Such faith on the part of even one person
in a community can uplift, can edify, can strengthen
and sustain the rest. It is a gift of great power.

Healing

It is the dream, the hope, the desire of every good
man to see evil dispelled from our world. Who does
not want to wipe away every tear from the Vietnamese
children, to feed the starving masses in India and
Africa, to return the diseased to health, to return the
dead to life? And yet we sit, appalled, day by day,
as poverty, ignorance and fear, war, violence and
hatred, starvation, sickness and anxiety surround and
at times seem to engulf us. We are tempted to ask if
we dare to hope for goodness, peace, health, and
happiness. But the Christian has every reason to hope.
The Christian who believes that on the cross Christ
reigns victorious over sin, death and evil must proclaim hope, release, and the Good News of salvation
to all the world. Our proclamation must not only be
abstract theory or pious platitudes. It must concretely
touch the troubled, sick and hungry men and give
peace, health, and release. The victorious life which
Christ made possible is not meant only for some
vague, shadowy, "somewhere" afterlife; it can be
known and lived in the sin-filled world of today.

It is not the purpose of the gift of healing to cure
all ills. There is no spiritual panacea. Jesus did not
cure all the hunger, pain, and trouble of his time.
Yet as a sign to all of salvation come to man by God,

he would often heal this paralytic or that deaf mute.
That seems to be the key to the gift of healing. Where
the Good News of Christ is proclaimed, a burst of
light from the sun of God's glory enters the darkness
of this world and a man is made whole. A sign is
raised for all to see. It is for this reason that we must
not openly reject the gift of healing. The fear is deep
in all of us that if we pray for healing and there is
no healing, then the whole reality is a "failure." But
we must wait for his sign-times. The Lord will provide
the occasions of his glory; we must provide the faith
to expect them.

Healing, total personal healing of the spiritual,
psychological, and physical man, is a gift the Lord
pours out upon his believing communities today.
The weight and memory of our whole tradition and
past training rose up to object most strenuously when
we first realized that we had to accept this, too, as a
present-day reality. And now we cannot object, for
like doubting Thomas we have seen, touched and
experienced the power of the Lord to heal—today.

No one can measure the number of internal healings the Lord has brought about as men and women
come to be renewed in his Spirit. Intimations were
given when relationships between people were healed
over. Indications were there as one man claimed that
the Lord had relieved him of a major obstacle to
grace with which he had been oppressed for many
years. And we got an inkling that a deep, personal,
healing had been accomplished when a boy who, in
his own words, "used to smile twice a semester,"
suddenly burst forth in a life of radiant, sustained
joy.

But concrete, physical healing has also become a

reality as a sign for all to see. One nun, who had received the baptism in the Spirit, suffered from a back injury caused by a fall. For some time she had worn a back brace, and she had been in traction three times. A number of doctors told her she would probably go through life with her movements quite restricted. She had trouble on stairs or when kneeling. In a prayer group one night she asked for prayers that she be healed. That night she took off the brace and has never worn it since.

—A priest who had been severely uncomfortable with a headache for several months was released from pain at the very moment he was being prayed for by some people who asked him if they might do so.

—A man with a chronic kidney condition and gout was healed of both illnesses and has not been troubled since.

Examples abound. Explain them as we will, individually and collectively they point to the reality of the risen Lord present among us in power. Not everyone who is prayed with for healing is healed visibly, but in our desire and hope to see all ills cured we pray; the Lord chooses his sign-times. For this we have come to believe that indeed "these signs shall attend those who believe ... they shall lay hands upon the sick and they shall get well ... The Lord ... was taken up into heaven and sits at the right hand of God. But they went forth and preached everywhere, while the Lord worked with them and confirmed the preaching by the signs that followed" (Mk. 16, 17-20).

Miracles

It is true that Jesus rebuked those who in challenging his authenticity were always "seeking a sign"

(Mt. 16, 4). If anything, the rebuke of our generation will be that we did not think to seek at all. Here, as with all the gifts of God, we will receive in proportion to our faith. Miracles do happen today. The visible, tangible, concrete, and divinely superfluous display of the power of God can be a reality in the life of the believer. These signs, usually in response to a prayer of expectant faith, are of value only insofar as they give evidence of the Good News of the Gospel, or insofar as they edify and build up the community of faith in the body of Christ.

Gift-miracles are intimately linked with the faith-gift. They are also linked closely at times to the gift of healing. These healings are indeed the more obvious miracles of our day. But are those which are less obvious, less miracles? Perhaps, yes, if by definition a miracle must be seen. But do we always see even that which is most obvious? When manna falls from the heavens, we say "Ah, a miracle!" But when, as happened to us some time ago, you have no food left in the house, it is Sunday and pay day has not yet come, and you pray for your "daily bread," is a telephone call from friends with a spur of the moment dinner invitation any less the fulfillment of your need simply because it seems so casual? Is the miracle of God's protection of his people stricken out of Exodus simply because an exegete says it was not a roaring sea but a shallow swamp that the people of God came through? The man of faith will see miracles everywhere the Lord touches, guides and heals his people. We will give you just a few examples from our experience.

Some minor miracles have occurred because we have dared, like Gideon (Jud. 6, 36-40) to lay a fleece before the Lord, because we dared to ask for a sign.

—Gerry Rauch, a Notre Dame graduate who has now chosen to live in poverty and work full time in religious counseling on college campuses, was hitchhiking one day from Michigan to a retreat being held in Indiana. It was late. There was little traffic. No one had stopped for him. And so he began to pray: "Lord if I am to go to this retreat, make it possible for me to get a ride within the next twenty cars. Thank you Lord. One...two..." The twentieth car slowed down, stopped. And before the ride to Indiana was through, he came to realize that not only had his "fleece" been taken care of by the Lord, but the man who stopped was a Pentecostal minister. One sign is added to another when you are looking for them.

—Our community at Notre Dame was searching for a relatively inexpensive apartment close to campus. Two young men, Jim Byrne and Pete Edwards, both graduates of Notre Dame, had decided to stay in what we have come to call "full time ministry" among the college students here. They needed a place to stay. As we prayed and looked, a gift-sign-miracle occurred. We suddenly found that an $18,000 house, fairly close to campus had been donated for our use by the owners to our community. We now have not only a place for Jim and Pete to stay, but a center, an axis, a home.

Each believer and community has experienced similar workings of the Lord. But the initial experience of the Pittsburgh community on the "Duquesne weekend" remains one of the most beautiful—and baffling. Dave Mangan tells the story this way:

"Upon returning to the house [after a walk] we received some startling news—we had no supply of water. Either the spring had dried up or the pump had broken, but we had no water. Then there were about five of us in the room and one of the leaders of the weekend asked us what we were going to do about it. Our reaction was, 'We can't do anything.' Then he suggested that we pray. At that time I really felt stupid. I felt like the apostles must have felt when they would make a dumb remark after being around Jesus. We collected some others and prayed. We became so sure that it was not God's will for us to go home yet that we prayed in thanksgiving for the water he was going to give us so we could stay. After we finished praying we went back to the normal course of events and expected results. In the early evening we had a bible vigil which was to be followed by a birthday party for three people present. About five minutes before the bible vigil I was struck with the realization that I was going to go downstairs and see the water. So immediately afterwards I went down into the kitchen and turned on the water. It was there with even more force than usual. What really surprised me was that I didn't even get excited. I just said to myself, 'Of course it's here; why shouldn't it be?' I walked out into the hall and announced that we had water. Those who had prayed with me (some didn't even know that the water was gone) were really joyful."

Explain it as you will, discuss degrees, probability, relativity and subjectivity, and you are still left with a conviction in the realm of faith that through faith on the part of his followers, through their human instrumentality, Jesus does work wonders in our day.

Prophecy

Unique and yet united to all the gifts of **utterance**

is prophecy. The everyday understanding of what it means to be a prophet is a sorry mixture of fortune telling and extra-sensory perception. Yet the notion of a prophet being one who predicts the future is far from biblical. The word "prophet" comes from the Hebrew *nabi* or the Greek *prophetes* which means "he who speaks for, or on behalf of." In this we see that a prophet reveals the future only insofar as he is like a weatherman. The weatherman looks at the present, deeply, knowingly, draws from past experience and can "see" that snow will fall tomorrow. In the gift of prophecy, an estimation of our religious situation necessarily involves an ability to know and to interpret the present deeply and to see in it the dynamism and the movement of the future. In the divine sphere this makes Jesus the prophet *par excellence,* for he is the supreme utterance, the perfect Word who speaks for the Godhead to us. He is the divine communication as human person. In him is all past, present and future; as Karl Rahner says:

"Though in him divine revelation has come to a close, prophets still have their para-institutional place in the Church, because ever and ever again there are people in the Church divinely sent to it to bear a personal testimony to the reality of God and Christ in the might of his Spirit."

This testimony is at times the embodied witness of a lifetime. These are the real prophets. Yet in this instance we are referring to prophetic utterance, to a word-gift given for a moment to an individual. The individual is not necessarily a prophet therefore, but he sometimes exercises a decided gift for prophecy, a gift for speaking out in the Lord's name as he is prompted. The word of prophecy is the word of the

Lord to a particular situation, perhaps to edify, encourage, console, or to teach, but always to ignite, enflame and enkindle. Prophetic utterance is meant to give a balance to the other Word-gifts. To the light of wisdom and knowledge, prophecy adds fire.

Since Jesus is *the* revelation of God to man, all prophecy, all teaching and all knowledge of him have their root and source of origin in the word of God. Scripture molds the content of any truly inspired utterance no matter what form it takes in being spoken. This is no doubt why the sound of "prophesying" from the mouth of an Evangelical Christian sounds strange to us. The message is the Lord's, but the medium is the King James Version of the bible. Therefore each sentence begins with "Yea I say unto thee" and usually ends with "Thus saith the Lord." In yielding to the prompting to speak forth a "prophetic" message, a Catholic in the same situation is more likely to use the language of contemporary texts. "Don't you know . . ." "The Lord would say," etc.

Forms through which the Lord would speak to us may be unfamiliar, but the authentic message from God will always ring true. How will we know? Are we sure it is the Lord? How can we test a genuine prophecy? Doesn't the weatherman make a mistake sometimes? In the spiritual realm, rain, when all signs point to sunshine, is most undesirable. The test of the prophetic utterance is found in its accord with the word of God.

> "Beloved, do not believe every spirit, but test the spirits to see whether they are of God; for many false prophets have gone out into the world. By this you know the Spirit of God: every spirit which confesses that Jesus Christ has come

in the flesh is of God, and every spirit which does not confess Jesus is not of God" (1 Jn. 4, 1-3). "Therefore I want you to understand that no one speaking by the Spirit of God ever says 'Jesus be cursed!' and no one can say 'Jesus is Lord' except by the Holy Spirit" (1 Cor. 12, 3). "'Beware of false prophets, who come to you in sheep's clothing but inwardly are ravenous wolves. You will know them by their fruits'" (Mt. 7, 15-16).

Discernment of Spirits

The interrelationships among the gifts again become obvious when we talk of "testing the spirits" of the prophets. Again it becomes clear that the Lord never gives a burdensome gift. Should the exercise of one gift raise problems, another gift is given to help.

The gift of "discernment" is not a propensity on the part of one person to tell everyone else just what is wrong with them. We have seen some harm done in the name of "discernment" over what was in actuality a "difference." We, for example, do not like the more emotional manifestations which occasionally accompany the working of the Lord in an individual. Laughing, crying, trembling—how immediately, how easily we want to say that it is not "of God." Perhaps it is not, but our judgment must come from the Lord and not be grounded merely on our tastes, likes, or preferences.

Contradiction in the life of the Spirit is impossible. We have already been warned by the Lord not to judge lest we ourselves be judged. True discernment is not merely a keen insight into the workings of our all too frail human nature. If this were the case only the psychologist would possess the gift. Discernment as a gift from God is the ability to distinguish at one moment in time whether the spirit behind a particular person, place, event, action, or situation is "of God" or not. It is obvious that if the work of God is to proceed, such a gift, acting as an agent of correction or counsel, is invaluable. We have seen that prudence and a great deal of care must be exercised by the individual who initially finds himself "aware" of these realities by the power of this gift. Holiness is no prerequisite to the reception of the gifts, nor is maturity. Yet where either is sorely lacking, the gifts can quickly become misused. In a community of love, this gift comes to take its place and perspective in the life in the Spirit.

The Gifts of Tongues and Interpretation

Disbelief and dispute concerning charismatic manifestations find focus all too often in the simple and yet dramatic gift of tongues. It is a convenient scapegoat for venting criticism and confusion. Speaking in tongues is a manner of prayer which, we believe, is meant to be a common, everyday occurrence in the life of the believing, Spirit-filled Christian. Yet at first glance it seems so uncommon, so extraordinary that its very mention evokes concern, curiosity, skepticism, and downright hostility. Because of this usual reaction, we felt it necessary to expand our consideration of this gift; the next chapter attempts to elaborate its meaning and purpose and to explain its significance. For the moment it should suffice to say that the gift of tongues is one of the word-gifts, an utterance of the Spirit through man, with one major difference. The other word-gifts are formed in the language of the one who speaks, while in this gift the speaker has no knowledge of the language in which he speaks. Form and content both are gifts of the Spirit. "And they were all filled with the Holy Spirit and began to speak in other tongues, as the Spirit gave them utterance" (Acts 2, 4).

Alone, the gift of tongues is used for prayer and praise. Coupled with the gift of interpretation it can edify the unbeliever and strengthen, console, enlighten or move the community of faith. Interpretation of tongues is a complimentary gift which is to be expected in the community. Without it the gift of tongues must remain in devotional, private use. "... If there is no one to interpret, let each of them [who would speak in tongues] keep silence in church and speak to himself and to God" (1 Cor. 14, 28).

The gift of interpretation is not a translation of a foreign language. Translation—the literal understanding of the words being spoken—has occurred in our groups, but this is not the gift of interpretation. To cite an instance of translation, Dave Mangan was once praying in tongues in Pittsburgh. A girl near him, a French major, was able partially to translate. Since she didn't understand some of it, she surmised it was an old dialect. A week later a Frenchman named Paul was in the group. After listening, he said Dave was speaking French, but not modern French. He said the accentuation of the various words and syllables was flawless. It takes an English-speaking person much time and practice to acquire. Dave, however, had no background in French.

—A man from Cleveland found one group of words very definitely forming and repeating every time he began to pray. He decided to try to transcribe or write down these sounds, the sentence which was always there when he began his prayer, to see if any language expert could discover what it was. He found that it was "The first Cause is my treasure"—a one-line prayer in Japanese.

—At a prayer meeting in South Bend, a priest who was attending his first prayer meeting asked the man next to him where he had learned Greek. Once again the answer was the same—"What Greek?" The priest then told the group that he had distinctly heard the man next to him repeat the opening lines of the "Hail Mary" in Greek during his prayer.

That occasion was a double gift from God. The meeting took, from that minute on, a decidedly Marian flavor. Prayer, discussion, and reflection centered on Mary as the type of all Christians who, overshadowed and empowered by the Spirit of God, brings Christ to the world. Those of us who are not too keen about excessive Marian devotion were still a bit disturbed after that meeting. We were a little apprehensive that the Spirit of God was not being served when the focus switched from Christ to Mary. But we worrywarts were confounded and joyful to discover that the next day was one of the greatest Marian feast days in the liturgical calendar. Our meeting the previous evening had not been a fearful diversion but an occasion. It had been a vigil, a preparation led by the Spirit for the feast that was to follow.

Interestingly enough in our experience, the person who was able to understand the language spoken was usually present as a critical observer, a skeptic. It seems as if these sign-gifts are given when the Spirit sees a need.

But it should be clear that this is not what we

mean by the gift of interpretation. In exercising interpretation as a gift of the Spirit, the language remains as foreign to the interpreter as to the one who speaks, yet the interpreter is given the sense, the meaning, the gist or impact of what is being spoken. It is not a word-by-word translation or comprehension; it ranges anywhere from a slight inkling to a total awareness, depending upon our openness, of what the Lord is trying to tell us. Receptivity to the exercise of this gift is a growth process. We must learn to act in faith, to speak out the first few, faint words which come to us. God will provide the rest.

These nine gifts, though not exclusive in the charismatic spectrum, are the specific manifestations of the Spirit which mark the renewal among us by a powerful confrontation with the Spirit of God. Their significance is best seen from the perspective of the worshiping community. It is in the liturgical framework that the reality and purpose of the gifts becomes defined. In the community experience of worship, the vertical dimension becomes obvious. The body of Christ is gathered, worships the Father, and the gifts become operative. This man is healed, that woman prophesies; not alone—it is the ministry, the continuation, the extension of the activity of Jesus in our midst. In this the gifts serve to build up the Church; and there is another level reaching out beyond any prayer group to embrace the world. In this horizontal dimension, the gifts serve as a sign to the world of the saving love of Jesus. It is the sacramentality, the corporeality of Jesus at work in his body. For the ambivalence, the mystery, the tension in any authentic Christian experience holds within itself the

symbol of the cross. Vertical and horizontal beams
unite to form the cross of Christ.

These gifts, given in the community, appropriated
by faith, come into community consciousness by their
exercise and the experience of them. The Spirit does
not give gifts that reside "up in the air" somewhere.
His gifts become incarnate, are present, are "poured
out" in his body and become operative through that
body when individuals meet to pray. It was in this
context of worship that Steve Clark first encountered
the operation of the gifts. We will let him describe
his initial reactions.

"It's new wine—life after the baptism in the Spirit.
And you can experience it in a prayer meeting in
which the gifts are operating. That's what we were
told. So we went. There was something different about
it right from the first. Something was indefinably
different. There was something going on in that room.
You could feel it. Everyone seemed expectant, as if
they were waiting for something to happen. There
was a leader, but he wasn't anything like a toast-
master. He was more like a conductor of an orchestra.
He gathered together, moderated, cued something that
everyone else was in on. It was as if everyone had
the score.

"The leader suggested a 'word' of prayer, and it
seemed like the prayer that was there already just
surfaced. All over the room people began to pray, at
first softly, then more and more loudly. To someone
accustomed to more orderly prayer it should have
seemed like babble, but there was a unity to it. It was
not confused. Everyone was praying together. We
began to hear a woman right behind us but we

couldn't understand what she was saying. Then it occurred to me that she must be praying in tongues. It sounded like Greek, musical and flowing. Soon I was able to pick out more people praying in tongues, each one saying something different. Then I had the courage to sneak a look to see what it all looked like. I soon discovered it didn't take much courage to look because no one paid much attention to me. Each person was absorbed in prayer. And it looked much like it sounded. Everyone was doing something different. Some sat, some stood. One man had his arms raised in a gesture of prayer. Yet throughout there was that same sense of unity.

"Then the prayer all of a sudden quieted down. After a moment someone spoke out loudly to the whole group. It must have been in a tongue. The 'message' lasted for a minute. Then, after a minute pause, someone else spoke out in English. He was in front of me and appeared perfectly calm. Not at all ecstatic. Yet he was speaking words from God, a message of consolation that almost sounded like a psalm. I knew that this must have been an interpretation of the tongue. After the interpretation, prayer broke out again, this time more joyfully. The man next to me was quietly saying 'thank you Jesus' over and over again. Then something even stranger happened. One by one they started to sing. Each person was singing a different melody and different words in, apparently, different languages. Yet the overall effect was beautiful and harmonious. This was singing in tongues, and there was no doubt, no question in my mind that it was worship. Prayer, singing, and worship went on into the evening. One man even stood up and gave a 'testimony' to his healing from crippling arthritis.

"When I went home and reread the twelfth chapter of First Corinthians, I saw a new meaning in the words of Saint Paul: 'When you come together, each one has a hymn, a lesson, a revelation, a tongue, or an interpretation. Let all things be done for edification.' Everyone was making a contribution; it was done with an unplanned spontaneity, each one adding what he had. All in all, there was no confusion, but rather a mysterious harmony. The new wine was a little strong for me, but I could see that it was good.

"I could see that something had been going on. This was something more than people doing just what they felt like. The speaking in tongues and prophecies seemed genuine. I was at least sure that people were not making them up. Since then, through experience, my perception of the reality of these things has grown. I have seen impressive healings . . . I have seen people's lives changed by the operation of these gifts. And I have experienced the greater awareness of God's presence that comes from the operation of these gifts in myself and others."

In this concrete and graphic way, Steve Clark encountered for the first time the living, twentieth century charisms, the gifts and fruits of the Spirit of God. His description of these gifts as exercised in the prayer meeting shows us in an existential dimension something of the nature of the gifts.

A person who has the spiritual gifts is not necessarily a holy person. He may even be spiritually immature or wayward. Christ recognized this when he said "Not every one who says to me, 'Lord, Lord,' will enter the kingdom of heaven, but he who does the will of my Father who is in heaven. On that day many will say to me 'Lord, Lord, did we not prophesy in your name and cast out demons in your name and do many mighty works in your name?' And then will I declare to them, 'I never knew you; depart from me you evildoers'" (Mt. 7, 21-23). He is not denying that they actually did these works, rather he is implying that they did. But he is saying that they are no guarantee of holiness.

Holiness and spiritual power unfortunately can be two separate things. A holy person is a person who does the will of the Father, who is given over to God. It is a personal quality. But a spiritual gift is equipment for the good of the Church. For many Catholics it is somewhat disconcerting to come across the spiritual gifts or to have to expect them as part of the normal Christian life. It is something all right for saints who lived far away in past ages, but not for here and now, and certainly not for my neighbor or myself. Gifts were so commonplace in the early Church, and came so frequently, that rules had to be formulated so they could be exercised in an orderly way. The Spirit is moving in his Church today, especially since the Second Vatican Council. Does it seem strange that we should expect a greater frequency of the spiritual gifts operative in the Church? Before the council we prayed every day: "Renew your wonders in this our day, as for a new Pentecost." We expected the council to be a "pentecostal" event, to be an outpouring of the Holy Spirit. It was. But the council is not over. Its impact is only now being felt, being lived, being incorporated.

The council Fathers gave us instructions on the

attitude we should take toward the spiritual gifts. "For the exercise of this apostolate, the Holy Spirit who sanctifies the People of God through the ministry and the sacraments gives to the faithful special gifts as well (cf. 1 Cor. 12, 7), 'allotting to everyone according as he will' (1 Cor. 12, 11). Thus may the individual, 'according to the gift that each has received, administer it to one another' and become 'good stewards of the manifold grace of God' (1 Pet. 4, 10), and build up thereby the whole body in charity (cf. Eph. 4, 16). From the reception of these charisms or gifts, including those which are less dramatic, there arise for each believer the right and duty to use them in the Church and in the world for the good of mankind and for the upbuilding of the Church. In so doing, believers need to enjoy the freedom of the Holy Spirit who 'breathes where he will' (Jn. 3, 8). At the same time, they must act in communion with their brothers in Christ, especially with their pastors. The latter must make a judgment about the true nature and proper use of these gifts, not in order to extinguish the Spirit, but to test all things and hold fast to what is good (cf. 1 Thess. 5, 12. 19. 21)" (*Decree on the Lay Apostolate,* n. 3).

The council teaches us that we should expect to see the gifts manifested, and it explains that the gifts are to be used primarily for the upbuilding of the Church, for the apostolate. They are intended as tools for our work as apostles.

Gifts are given to an individual that he may grow in the fruit of the Spirit. The fruit of the spirit is charity, joy, peace, patience, kindness, goodness, faith, modesty, continency. The fruit of the spirit is the harvest of God's sowing within an individual. The fruit of the Spirit are the characteristics of Jesus. Growth in the fruit of the Spirit given in abundance as a result of the baptism in the Spirit conforms an individual to Christ. For to possess the fruits of the Spirit is to be Christlike.

Again and again as individuals give witness to what Christian life became for them after the baptism in the Spirit, the words love, joy and peace spring up within them. As Father Edward O'Connor noted in *Ave Maria* magazine, "whatever other particular effects may have occurred, peace and joy seem to have been received by all, almost without exception, of those who have been touched by the Spirit. These two terms rise almost unfailingly to the lips of anyone who gives testimony to what the Lord has done for him. The peace is deeper than any they have ever known; the joy wells up from within like a fountain that is ever fresh, and yet it is without the exuberance or elation that makes human joy liable to excess and then deflation."

In the initial confrontation with the Spirit in power, brilliant intimations, foretastes of the glory of the Christian life, are poured out abundantly. Signs abound. The Lord has worked here. But as we begin to walk in this life of the Spirit, we are inexperienced, childlike, green. The good fruit by which the Spirit would have himself manifest in us needs time to ripen, to grow, to develop in an organic way.

The real test of our receptivity, of our response and conformity to Christ, lies in the day-to-day existence which follows our "mountain top" experience. It is here, in the nitty-gritty, mundane, tension-filled activities of life that we can choose to stunt all growth or to develop, to come to a mature life in Christ that yields abundant fruit.

Peace, joy, patience, how easily they come to us and flow from us in the center of a prayer meeting where faith is strong. But during the next day, the next headache, the next crisis with our neighbor, husband, boss, roommate, or pastor—it is here that life in Christ becomes our all or our nothing. In a letter to Jim Byrne, Mary McKendrick of Michigan State expressed her personal discovery of these truths:

"Dear Jim,

"Grace and peace to you in the name of our Lord, Jesus Christ. This is going to be a joyous letter—even if we at Michigan State did just lose the football game to you Notre Dame people. I talked to Bob last night and he said he'd received a letter from you. It's good to know that you're still alive. I was beginning to wonder. Seriously, I've often thought of you—we all have—and have been wondering how everything is going for you and the whole community at Notre Dame.

"God has really been good to all of us here. Most people continue to grow in leaps and bounds, and it's such a fantastically beautiful thing to see. God is so good to us! One person's strength combats and complements another's weakness. We can all really help each other to grow in the Lord, and in return, he brings us so much closer together. We receive so very, very much in return for what we give to him.

"God has really been teaching and guiding me this term. He keeps showing me my weaknesses, and sometimes it can really be a humiliation—but what joy there is when I suddenly realize what he's done. I have never been so aware of his presence before. I have also never been so aware of how many times I turn away or deny him—and yet he is always there loving and forgiving and giving hope. Do you remember that during the week we spent at Notre Dame I told you that I'd suddenly realized I hadn't cried for six months or so? It was quite a shock, and I spent a lot of time trying to psych myself out and figure out what was the matter with me. One day I suddenly realized that not crying was a sign of something much bigger. I have always been one big emotion, and I'm not anymore. The Holy Spirit has taught me a peace that I had never known existed. He has taught me to control myself and he has also shown me what is important and what is not. I don't cry. I don't cry anymore, that is, when someone looks at me cross-eyed or says something nasty to me. I've discovered that religion and God are not just emotional experiences. Before the baptism in the Holy Spirit my only real encounters not only with Christians but also with Christ had been very emotional, like on weekends. You're on Cloud Nine for a few days and then Wham! You hit earth again. I know now that living with Christ isn't a Cloud Nine-type experience. It involves living every minute of every day with him and for him. That's not always easy—my 'flesh' wants to fight too often. And yet I know he's always with me! Wow! That's saying quite a lot. If my encounters with Christ were only emotional they would be only superficial because you can't live on emotions every minute of your life. That's too unreal and I know it. I guess what I'm trying to say is that before the baptism in the Spirit I had kind of believed that in order to know Christ you had to feel something good all the time. If I didn't feel good when I was praying then I thought God wasn't there or that something was drastically the matter with me. Of course there were plenty of times when I didn't feel anything when I was praying, so I just kind of gave up. I really thank God that he has taught me that living with Christ is like marriage after the honeymoon. You have to settle down to the hard work of living with each other and getting used to being together all the time. You have to learn that loving means giving completely of yourself, even in all the little things. For us, it means dying to ourselves and living in Christ.

"I will close now by asking you to pray for us here in East Lansing and we will remember you in our prayers. Praise the Lord always and may God continue to bless you. Yours in Christ, Mary."

The fruit of the Spirit is given to be a sign here in the midst of life so that peace, joy, faith, kindness, and patience are possible in this world. The fruit of the Spirit is the mark of a Christian. One sign above all others clearly gave evidence to a life lived for Jesus in the early Church. Everyone marvelled: "See how they love one another." Love, the first fruit of the Spirit holds within itself all that Christianity is meant to be. All gifts will pass away, but love alone remains, for God is love—and he who abides in love abides in God, and God abides in him (1 Jn. 4, 16).

We would like to try to summarize all that we have tried to say about the significance of the charismatic gifts of the Spirit and the fruit they bear. The rapid spread of what is usually termed "secularity" among men in contemporary society is by now a fact. It is alarming to some, understandable to many. Its cause is debated quite regularly in academic circles. But one thing seems clear: There has been a remarkable failure on the part of institutional Christianity, Catholic and Protestant alike, to speak a relevant word of salvation to modern man. Men today are not interested in pious practices or abstract virtue. Where Christianity is a part of the fiber of the society as an establishment, where the nation goes to church but the Sunday dose of spiritual medicine wears off in Monday's marketplace, faith is dead. A God may indeed be worshipped here, but he is faceless and abstract. He is not the Father of our Lord, Jesus Christ.

The idealistic young, the "secular" theologians, the "hippies," the "man in the street" all seem to be crying out: "Down with pretty music and pious preaching; let us love one another right now!" Christian witness if it is to survive, if it is to be Christian, must be humanly concerned. It must be truly loving. It must be Christ.

We believe the baptism in the Holy Spirit with these dynamic gifts and fruit speaks radically to the secular man. They meet him where he is, where he lives. Through these gifts Jesus heals him, consoles him, and loves him. No theological explanation is necessary to see that kindness, love, and gentleness answer precisely the craving for authentic, loving, interpersonal relationships that alone will make our societies whole.

The life of the Spirit, gifts and fruit, is not an abstract, otherworldly thing. It is radically incarnational. Jesus dealt with men and women in their real, everyday situations. With all their anxieties and problems, he loved them and transformed them. **The gifts and fruit of the Spirit alive in the Body of**

Christ are meant to be and to do precisely the same love-action today.

For the Holy Spirit, the enlivening, personal power of God in the Church, exists in the Church today not as the unknown member of the Trinity, not only as an intellectual light switched on in times of decision, not only as a strange symbol in religious art, or an impersonal dove flapping feathered wings, but in the same dynamic and powerful way he operated in the apostolic Church. He comes upon those who take Christ at his word and wait for the Spirit he will send. He comes with an array of gifts to build up the Church, to make it strong, to make of it a love-sign-gift, and to enable it as fully as possible to be the great sacrament of Christ in the world.

6

Speaking in Tongues

... These gifts include charity, wisdom, faith, prophecy, healing, discernment of spirits, speaking in tongues, and interpretation of tongues. But it is tongues—considered to be the least of the Holy Spirit's gifts—that has received the most attention.

When a person speaks in tongues his speech is said to be triggered into praising God in a foreign language unknown to the speaker or in a flow of indiscernible syllables.

The National Catholic Reporter

"My ways are not your ways." Of all the truths in the word of God, this quotation aptly describes the experience most commonly related with the baptism in the Holy Spirit—"speaking in tongues." "Ridiculous ... absurd ... bizarre ... unnecessary ... irrational"—every conceivable objection we could mouth was formed to refute the necessity and reality of praying in an unknown tongue. In the natural order of our way of relating to God there was no more humanly repulsive thought than to speak what we felt would be gibberish. But our ways of wisdom are not always his.

Though it will be necessary to explain exactly *what* we mean by "speaking in tongues," or glossalalia, might we not first ask *why* speak in tongues at all? In poetry, music, art, and in so many other ways we try to reach beyond ourselves, to express the inexpressible, to hymn the beauty, the rapture, and even the inevitable ugliness of the world of God's creation. Lovers in the silent depths of wordless glances speak a language only they can hear. In moments, rare moments of intensity "too deep for tears" or too exhalted for feeble words, we have known the need, the cry of our beings to create expression, response. If ever words were inadequate it is in the presence of the Word who loves and calls and evokes from us our all. To him be glory and praise forever! "Praise him for his mighty deeds; praise him according to his exceeding greatness! Praise him with trumpet sound; praise him with the lute and harp! Praise him with timbrel and dance; praise him with strings and pipe! Praise him with sounding cymbals; praise him with loud clashing cymbals! Let everything that breathes praise the Lord!" (Ps. 150). In this way the psalmist cries out his Amen to the glory of God. This is the *why* of speaking or praying in tongues. "Tongues" is not an emotional evocation of an experience. Rather its nature is response. It is the child's delight, the glee that greets the fireworks display on the Fourth of July, not the display itself.

To describe *what* is meant by speaking in tongues, we must turn first to the Acts of the Apostles, chapter two: "When the day of Pentecost had come, they were all together in one place. And suddenly a sound came from heaven like the rush of a mighty wind, and it filled all the house where they were sitting. And there appeared to them tongues as of fire, distributed and resting on each one of them. And they were all filled with the Holy Spirit and began to speak in other tongues, as the Spirit gave them utterance" (Acts 2, 1-4). Time and time again, this "evidence" appears when scripture speaks of a deep working of the Holy Spirit in the lives of the early Christians. This is true not only on the day of Pentecost but as normative in the faith-life which formed the various communities. It is mentioned also in chapter 19 of Acts, verses 6 and 7: "And when Paul had laid his hands upon them, the Holy Spirit came on them; and they spoke with tongues and prophesied." Again, in chapter 10 of Acts, the believers who were with Peter noted with amazement that "the Holy Spirit had been poured out even on the Gentiles. For they heard them speaking in tongues and extolling God." We do not like to call this an "evidence" of the infilling of the Spirit. For certainly one can be filled by the Spirit without the tangible evidence of tongues. Yet from a powerful and expectant confrontation with the Spirit of the Lord the gift of tongues emerges again and again if not as an "evidence" certainly as a "consequence" in the lives of many Christians.

Is it biblical fundamentalism to see an application for today in these texts? Even if we grant that the events did happen in the first century, does it mean they still can happen in the twentieth? In citing these controversial pentecostal texts, it is important to note that we see in them an authoritative witness of the early Christian community to the action of the Spirit. We cite them here as "faith texts," not as an attempted apologetic. "Passage picking" to argue and prove points from scripture serves no purpose. That method of refutation and that era of argument are over. If contemporary scriptural exegesis has shown us anything it is that each saying, each event, must be considered a part of the whole fabric or context in which it is placed. Anything less is radical fundamentalism which denies the instrumentality, culture, and consciousness of the human experience of faith which formed these texts in the post-resurrection community.

On the intellectual level, we leave it to the scholars and exegetes to determine how much allegorical, imagistic or midrashic elements combine to form the pentecostal theme in Acts. We leave it to the scholars and exegetes to determine whether or not glossalalia should be classified as ecstatic utterance or unintelligible language. We leave it to the scholars and exegetes to determine whether or not glossalalia as described in Acts or First Corinthians is a related phenomenon to the ecstatic speech of other Oriental religions, or of Hellenistic religion, or whether it is a new phenomenon or experience. Yet on the level of faith, we must claim with R. H. Gundry that to the Christian community at that time "the effectiveness of glossalalia as an authenticating sign . . . depended on its *difference* from the ecstatic gobbledegook in Hellenistic religion." It also seems that the current game of demythologizing glossalalia to the point of meaning merely powerful and persuasive oratorical speech has, in fact, no intellectual or historical foundation even in the most Bultmannian exegesis. Nor does it seem wise, in the realm of faith, to reduce the significance of the "speaking in tongues" or the entire Pentecost account to the level of mass hysteria (as is done by C. S. Mann in an appendix to the commentary on Acts in the *Anchor Bible*). The credibility of the community inspired to transmit the Gospel of the Lord Jesus becomes rather tenuous under this form of *a priori* analysis.

Once we concede that the reality of glossalalia can be admitted, we must ask whether it is necessary. What good is it to speak in tongues?

Second only to biblical fundamentalism, love, it would seem, is the major reason offered for a rejection of glossalalia in the Christian life. Using First Corinthians, the external phenomena of the charismata are denied importance. "If I should speak with the tongues of men and of angels, but do not have charity, I have become as sounding brass and tinkling cymbals." With this the critic is apt to say, "Keep your charisms, they have never fed one hungry orphan or loved one neglected person." Yet is this true? If all charisms are by nature directed to the building up of the body of Christ, it must benefit others if I "speak in tongues." What are the purposes of glossalalia? How is it essentially oriented to the service of others? In what sense is it an exercise of love?

If we continued reading the words of Saint Paul on love we will find him exhorting us to "Make love your aim, *and* earnestly desire the spiritual gifts." (Italics added.) The exercise of all the charismatic gifts is essentially a ministry of love, edification, upbuilding, and deliverance. In the case of the gift of healing this should be particularly evident since it has results in the tangible physical realm. Yet when scripture speaks of the power of prayer in tongues, we are not so immediately convinced of its love and deliverance. "But in like manner, the Spirit also helps our weakness. For we do not know what we should pray for as we ought, but the Spirit himself pleads for us with unutterable groanings" (Rom. 8, 26-28). In tongues we find the words the Lord would have us pray, and through them we find deliverance. Powerful examples of this kind of deliverance abound in a book about a young Pentecostal minister and his work with teenage dope addicts in Brooklyn—*The Cross and the Switchblade* by David Wilkerson. One of the boys who was cured of dope addiction through the baptism in the Holy Spirit describes the importance of the experience, of his new ability to pray in tongues, of his new relationship to Jesus:

"... He helped me to get rid of drugs. I used goof balls and marijuana, and I was beginning to skin pop heroin. I already had the mind habit and I had to do this thing. When I heard about Jesus it kind of shocked me that He loved people in spite of all their sins. It stirred me when I heard that He puts real teeth behind His promises by coming into us with this Baptism in the Holy Spirit. The Holy Spirit is called the Comforter they told me. When I thought of comfort I thought of a bottle of wine and half-a-dozen goofballs. But these guys were talking about comfort out of Heaven where I could feel clean later.

"So I got to wanting this ... In the chapel ... I cried to God for help, and that's when He came around. He took over my lips and tongue and I was speaking in a new language. At first I thought I was crazy, but all of a sudden I knew I couldn't be because something was happening too. I wasn't lonely anymore. I didn't want any more drugs. I loved everybody. For the first time in my life I felt clean."

What is most important for us in this testimony is the realization that even when "tongues" itself is not being used in the service of others, the renewed faith-life still gives a new or renewed zeal to serve Jesus in his body. The new world of Christian concern that is released by the encounter with the Spirit —of which tongues is a concrete, tangible sign—has love as both root and fruit.

It helps to repeat again and again if necessary, that it is not the purpose of the baptism in the Holy Spirit to spread the gift of tongues, but rather to deepen the Christian's relationship of love with God and man, in and through Christ. The center of this activity is Christ, and it is to him, not to tongues or healing or prophecy, that we wish to witness. When these things accompany an intensification of faith-life as they have among us then we praise God for them, for they are truly gifts and real helps to the Christian community. But in themselves, or separated from the person of Christ or from the love which he commands us to have toward all men, they are nothing and worthless. Their origin is in Christ, and their purpose is to build up and to edify others who with us form his Body in the world today.

Many orphans have been fed and many neglected persons loved through the social work apostolate and in the exercise of the traditional corporal works of mercy. But persons have been helped also through the exercise of the charismatic gifts—tongues included. The power of prayer to the believing Christian is limitless. "And my God will supply every need of yours according to his riches in glory in Christ Jesus" (Phil. 4, 19). "Therefore I tell you, whatever you ask in prayer, believe that you will receive it, and you will" (Mk. 11, 24). "If you abide in me, and if my words abide in you, ask whatever you will and it shall be done for you" (Jn. 15, 7). "And whatever you ask in prayer, you will receive if you have faith" (Mt. 21, 22). And Jesus has said: "All things are possible to him who believes" (Mk. 9, 23). The impact of these promises found in the word of God is indeed staggering. In humility our response should parallel that of the father of the possessed boy in Mark's gospel: "Immediately the father of the boy cried out, and said with tears, 'I believe, help my unbelief'" (Mk. 9, 24).

Petition on behalf of another, therefore, is the first of the many "uses" or "purposes" of the gift of tongues. Coupled with the gifts of interpretation (1 Cor. 12, 10) the public message spoken in tongues to the community has yet another purpose—edification to the unbeliever. An unbeliever in our understanding need not only be the atheist; even an extremely dedicated Christian can be an unbeliever when it comes to the manifestations of the Spirit. One such "believing unbeliever" (a nun who was in summer school at Notre Dame in 1967) later wrote us her impressions of the gift of tongues. Its edification purpose seems to have been served:

"In regard to the 'unknown tongues,' a musically trained mind and ear, accustomed to hearing rhythms and nuances, accustomed to analyzing tonal patterns, repetitions, and balances, unconsciously seeks and discerns structures of audial forms. The identifying parallels between patterns of sound in the tongues and those in the interpretations or translations which invariably followed when tongues were spoken in the assembly were sometimes quite apparent. These were usually little poetic, psalmlike gems of praise or prophecy (in the broad sense of the word, 'to speak out on behalf of') ; the theological content was beyond reproach—praise directed to God the Father, with and through the Son, in the power and leading of the Holy

Spirit. To one conscious of the wonders of creation who loves to contemplate the heavens, there is no scandal or difficulty in accepting (perhaps even understanding why) that the Holy Spirit might want to perfect praise in this way—out of the mouths of babes. For indeed the ones moved to speak in unknown tongues were using none of their own adult talent, learning, wisdom, or ingenuity. They were closer to being like children learning by imitation and repetition, than to any mature adult formulation. At the same time the prayers uttered in this manner were gems of poetic composition and content—too much so to have been composed on the spur of the moment by amateurs."

Yet if tongues serves any purpose at all, it is not in the realm of petition or of edification or of public prayer that we will find the fundamental, essential, and ultimate "use" of this gift. It is in praise! "For one who speaks in a tongue speaks not to men but to God, for no one understands him, but he utters mysteries in the Spirit" (1 Cor. 14, 2). This is why it is stressed that tongues is not evocative; it is in the nature of a response, a loving response to the wonder and glory of God who in his lavish generosity gives us not only his Son, his love, his life, but even the gift of words with which to thank him. "For out of the abundance of the heart the mouth speaks" (Mt. 12, 34). Praise of God, spontaneous, overflowing, heartfelt praise of the Lord, not for anything he has done for us but just praise for being who he is (or he-who-is), this kind of praise did not come easily to us before baptism in the Spirit. Yes, we knew that praise was a higher form of prayer, and petition supposedly the lowest, yet our felt need was easier to verbalize in prayer than was our experience of the greatness of God. Only in praying the psalms had we occasionally been quickened by an awareness of God's glory. With the baptism in the Holy Spirit— particularly with the gift of tongues which is essentially a gift of praise—a newer, deeper, and more joyous ability for prayer of praise became evident. Two minutes of prayer in tongues can make ten minutes of intelligible praise in English possible, and richer.

Jim Cavnar summed it up this way: ". . . One of the men came over and laid his hands on me. I found myself speaking in tongues so fluently and quickly that I knew it was not just something I was doing on my own. The tongues were also accompanied with a strong feeling of the love of God and a great desire to praise him.

"Praising God was something that I had always known was important to Christian prayer, but I had never felt much like doing it before. Whatever it meant to 'praise' God was unclear to me. But tongues taught me to praise God, giving me such an awareness of his greatness and love that I would feel naturally and spontaneously drawn to praise him, especially in tongues since it seemed to express desires of my heart that my English was frustrated to express."

In Jim's description, his reception of the gift of tongues is immediate and fluent. Not everyone who receives does so in the same way. Some people find there is a delay of an hour, a week, or more. When Tom Noe received the baptism in the Holy Spirit, there was no immediate manifestation, ". . . but the absence of tongues didn't worry me. I had felt too much of the overwhelming presence of God to be concerned that I still had to praise and thank him in English. About two and one half weeks later, I was sitting waiting for theology class to start. I was using the time to pray the rosary, a practice I had taken up since the baptism. There were several others in the room also waiting, and so I prayed silently, moving my lips to the prayers. I was very quiet and meditative throughout, and the only 'out of the ordinary thing' that happened was that after I finished the last prayer my lips decided to keep moving and rearranged themselves into a confusion of p's, k's, and l's. I was just about to start speaking out loud in tongues when I remembered that there were 'ignorant' bystanders around who might be quite upset to witness such an outburst, so I thought, 'Stop,' and notwithstanding the immense sense of joy and happiness of closeness to God that made me want to raise my arms in the air and shout out the glory of God, I made it through the class. One thing though: I was naturally grinning broadly, and the teacher was quite disturbed to have one of his students ignore his lecture and grin steadily at him for an entire class period. Later that day I first used my 'tongue' in prayer and it has since become a valuable part of my entire prayer experience."

One young man, Phil Orth from Elwood, Ind., yielded to tongues while he was sound asleep after a prayer meeting one night. It was quite unconscious. He was home on vacation and the door to his room was ajar—his mother heard him speaking—but it was a language she did not understand. When she told him what she had heard, he praised God for the news and was able to release the gift consciously in prayer that day. The way in which this gift is received seems to be as varied as the individuals who ask for it in bold and expectant faith. Though such faith is needed to receive tongues, it is also evident that faith is strengthened in yielding to tongues.

It is a common rule of thumb in the realm of the Spirit that once an advance has been made by one of God's sons, the archenemy of the Lord (we still believe in him too) is even more diligent in his attempts to evoke doubt and rejection of this new grace, this new awareness of the power of Jesus. Since the subtle workings of the Spirit lend themselves to human instrumentality (in prayer in tongues, it is we who speak), a common fear is that it is *only* we who speak. The day after one of our group at Notre Dame received the gift of tongues she went to school to teach as usual, but with great joy. But as the day wore on, memories of the initial step of faith in receiving the new gift of praise from the Father came in tinged with fear and doubt. Would it last, was it real? As she explained it: "The students had all gone to lunch. The hallway was finally quiet. I slipped into the chapel. Shadows from the stained glass chapel windows sent rainbows to play around the altar. I knelt, looking carefully around once more. All clear. Slowly, haltingly it came again, the rhythms of the language that I did not know. It was the 'morning after the night before,' but there in the school chapel I dared again to speak in faith the strange yet haunting syllables of praise. Whispers turned to bold, strong words and with each word my last faint fears were gone. A new faith in Jesus took root."

Even the most innocent expressions used to relate an experience can easily fall prey to extensive analysis in this age of psychological understanding. It is obvious that some of the expressions we have just used ("tongues . . . seemed to express desires . . . English was frustrated to express"; he "yielded to tongues [unconsciously] while he was sound asleep") do tend to open wide the critical eye of the amateur and professional psychologist. Indeed the entire pentecostal experience has been labeled by some as "fanatic" or "crackpot." For those who wish to couch a label in more subtle terminology, expressions like "enthusiasm," "emotionalism," or "quaint cultic rite" serve the purpose equally well of reducing a valid psychological objection, a valid psychological questioning, to the level of uncritical rejection.

We would like to look very briefly at the psychological implications and/or problems that the experience of the manifestations of the baptism in the Holy Spirit bring to the surface. Because of the incarnation of Jesus Christ we can learn from, grow in, and integrate the psychological dimensions of religious experience within the human person.

As Henri Nouwen, visiting professor of psychology at Notre Dame, has said: "More and more it has become clear that God reveals himself to man through man and his world and that a deeper understanding of human behavior leads us to a deeper understanding of God. The new insights of psychology, sociology, anthropology . . . are no longer feared as possible threats to the supernatural God, but more as an invitation to theological reflection on the new insights and understanding."

Amateur "psychologizers" among us one day were trying to find the psychological "mechanism" behind tongues. It is easy to conclude that glossalalia is "nothing but" the releasing of an unconscious or

preconscious world of meanings in repetitive tones
different in each person, since each personality repre-
sents a different constellation of meaning. This could
be an explanation of the phenomenon. It sounds good
to us. There could be any number of explanations for
the phenomenon. But does the availability of natural
causation deny divine initiative? Our position on this
is best stated by the nun whom we have referred to as
our "unbelieving-believer":

"Of course a depth psychologist may have terms
to explain the whole thing on a purely natural level.
This kindly, peaceful, stimulating experience of being loved in community calls on the natural healing
powers of the psyche to become activated. But then
the Spirit does not reject the instrumentation of natural powers, nor does the Church's sacramental
system. The same God is the author of all."

Since the incarnation of Christ there is no radical
dichotomy possible between the supposedly natural
and the supposedly supernatural. The Christian perspective sees all things transformed in Christ. Without
the acceptance of God in Christ, analysis of religious
experience can lead one to say "it is nothing but
this or that." Karl Stern in his book dealing with
psychiatry and religion, *The Third Revolution,* shows
the pitfall in this line of reasoning most clearly:

"If there were nothing beyond the psychological,
all the saints from Simeon Stylites to the Poverello,
to Benedict Joseph Labre, to Thérèse of Lisieux,
would indeed make up a fools' parade. Yet there is
no area in which the 'nothing but,' the reductive
principle, is more absurd than the life of the spirit.
Under that aspect the spirit evaporates, and life itself
becomes reduced to a desiccated specimen ... We have

to admit one thing: the psychological plane and the spiritual plane are not independent of each other. On the contrary, they are most intimately connected.

"Consider the following example. Helene Deutsch in discussing Saint Bernadette Soubirous observes why little Bernadette came to see the 'Lady,' at the time of her original vision. She analyzes little Bernadette's relationship to her mother, to the remaining children of the family, the actual situation on the day of the first apparition, particularly the role of Bernadette's sister who had waded across the river before Bernadette. Finally the psychoanalyst speaks of the symbolic significance of the cold rushing river and the 'Lady.' One can say, as Helene Deutsch does, that the child's inner constellation was such that at the moment she had to produce a hallucinatory Great Mother. This psychoanalytic interpretation is probably quite correct, though it says nothing about the question of the reality of the apparition. If nothing exists beyond the psychological, it is the only possible explanation. If something else does exist, as every Christian believes, there is another explanation: suppose the Blessed Virgin were to choose a certain time and place to appear; would she not choose a girl who was, on the natural plane, best prepared for the encounter? Would she not choose someone whose psychological constellation was such that it offered a natural response? One has to be 'hungry' to be filled by God 'with good things' (Lk. 1, 53). 'I have to decrease so that you may increase.' This is a principle which one can discover at every step along the history of salvation. The election did not go to the mighty Egyptians, but to a little tribe of slaves—just the sort of people who might have dreamed up the story of special election—it is the sort of myth you would expect them to come up with, as a 'compensation' for their humiliation. And so it goes, all the way down to the weak and enslaved people of the Roman imperial time who, according to Nietzsche, had to invent a shackled and suffering God in order to extol the state in which they found themselves. That extraordinary neediness, that specific frustration of those to whom the revelation comes—that is a very real sign throughout the entire Judaeo-Christian history. It is the sign of paradox which marks the divine encounter.

"On the other hand, since Nietzsche, this very fact has become the psychological temptation *par excellence*. It is one very particular aspect of the 'nothing but.' If one scrutinizes the life history of any saint or of any mystic carefully enough, one will always find the psychological reason why the supernatural happened when it happened. When God comes into our life, He 'comes in handy.' To those who think exclusively in psychological terms, this makes the supernatural experience suspect. At the same time it explains the initial caution of the Church when she is confronted with such phenomena as the apparitions of little Bernadette. In the last analysis, there is only one perfectly reliable criterion. It is, by their fruits you shall know them."

Glossalalia, the gift of tongues, the gift of prayer and praise is in fact meant to be, we believe, a normal experience for all Christians. It is not meant for an elite; it is not meant only for those who like a little emotion charged into their religion. Prayer in tongues need not be overly emotional. We can't call it unemotional, for as body-persons all our human experiences are unified. The mind, the soul, the body, the emotions are never compartmentalized. If we were unemotional we would be dead. If the kind of "tongues" normally demonstrated among fundamentalist pentecostals in the last seventy years has often been ecstatic, supercharged with emotionalism, can't these characteristics be traced to the cultural context of revivalism rather than to the gift of tongues itself?

Father Edward O'Connor noted that "the one who speaks in tongues is aware that he is praying to God or praising him, but not of the exact meaning of what he says. He speaks according to the prompting or guidance of a force within him that does not come from himself; yet he is conscious that he himself does the speaking, and he remains free to begin and quit when he sees fit. There is nothing ecstatic about the experience. The subject is perfectly calm and in full command of his senses; he is aware of what he is doing and of what goes on around him. Frequently he is engaged in a normal, rational conversation immediately before and after the speaking in tongues."

While we believe that charisms are meant to be normative for Christian behavior, we do not mean to imply that Christian behavior will always seem "normal." There is always something "abnormal" about faith. Turning once more to Karl Stern: "There always remains an element of madness in the spiritual encounter ... Whenever in the history of revelation man and God meet face to face, as it were, something happens which is not at all normal. This is the sign of paradox which marks the entire story of revelation ... God loves man with the madness of love, and he tries man's love to the point of madness."

It may seem mad to pray in tongues. It may seem foolish. But perhaps, we, like Saint Paul, must be ready to be "fools" for Christ.

John Sherrill, in his book, *They Speak With Other Tongues,* has an anecdote which best sums up the attitude we believe everyone should have toward the gift of praising God in tongues:

"'I think the mistake is to divorce tongues from the essential whole of which they are a part,' said Dr. Ervin [a Baptist minister in Atlantic Highlands, New Jersey]. 'Let me tell you a little story. I happen to be fond of church architecture. One day when I was out driving I found an exquisite little Gothic chapel. I stopped my car and got out to admire it.

"'But that little church happened to have at its entrance a bright, red door. My eyes would try to follow the soaring lines of the building upward as Gothic architecture makes you do, but every time they were jerked back to that red door. It was so flamboyant it kept me from seeing the whole picture.

"'Tongues, John, are like that door. As long as you stand outside your attention is going to be riveted there and you're not going to be able to see anything else. Once you go through, however, you are surrounded by the thousand wonders of light and sound and form that the architect intended. You look around and that door isn't even red on the inside. It's there. It's to be used. But it has taken its proper place in the design of the whole church.

"'That's what I'd hope for you, John, I think it's time for you to walk through that door. If you really want to discover what the pentecostal experience is all about, don't concentrate on tongues, but step through the door and meet the Holy Spirit.'"

7

Walking in the Spirit

What was to be another five-hour meeting got underway with a couple of standard prayers and hymns. Then followed the scripture reading and individuals witnessing to the inspiration of the Spirit in their lives. They told how they had overcome this problem or that animosity, how they had suddenly experienced what it really means to love God.

There seemed to be no barriers, no inhibitions. No grim Sunday faces isolating their glances by staring into black-bound prayer books. They sat cross legged on the floor. Ladies in slacks. White-robed monk. Cigarette smokers. Coffee drinkers. Praying in free-form, singing loudly to drown out a baby crying at the other end of the house. It occurred to me that these people were having a good time praying! Is this what they meant by the Holy Spirit dwelling amongst them?

The National Catholic Reporter

The living room assembly meets to share the day-in day-out life after the baptism in the Holy Spirit. Here is sustained joy, continuing good results and ongoing worship in love. It is here that we discover what is deeper than one prayer experience, what unites the exercise of the various ministry gifts. It is here that we listen and hear the continual affirmation, the Yes to Jesus. Here is the continual response to the voice of the Spirit calling and dwelling deeply within.

"If I speak in tongues of men and of angels, but have not love, I am a noisy gong or a clanging cymbal. And if I have prophetic powers, and understand all mysteries, and all knowledge, and if I have all faith, so as to remove mountains, but have not love, I am nothing. If I give away all I have, and if I deliver my body to be burned, but have not love, I gain nothing" (1 Cor. 13, 1-4).

"But the fruit of the Spirit is love, joy, peace, patience, kindness, goodness, faithfulness, gentleness, self-control; against such there is no law. And those who belong to Christ Jesus have crucified the flesh with its passions and desires. If we live by the Spirit, let us also walk by the Spirit. Let us have no self-conceit, no provoking of one another, no envy of one another" (Gal. 5, 22-25).

The often-repeated words from two of Saint Paul's letters have a most important message for Christians, especially for anyone interested in the charismatic renewal. In the context of the Catholic pentecostal movement, our brother Paul is laying it on the line: You can have all the gifts of the Spirit in the world, but if they don't lead to the fruit of the Spirit, forget it. Now the fruit of the Spirit is love. Many other qualities, attributes of Christ, are meant to be characteristics of the relationships among Christians. Gifts can be given in a minute, but it takes time to grow fruit. As fruit grows it improves, it gets better. Any fruit grower can improve his product by pruning, grafting, and caring for his trees. Good fruit is the product of a process of growth and development just as human life is a process of growth and development.

Thus for us to live by the Spirit is not a one-moment event, nor is it just the reception of a special gift. It is a walk in the Spirit, a process, a journey, a pilgrimage. It is the task of Christian life in the world. It is also the joy of Christian life in the world.

We have discussed the history, theology and effect of the baptism in the Holy Spirit. To you it may sound so wonderful that you would like to share in it. Or it may be attractive, but you have your suspicions. Perhaps it seems all too sudden, as if the change from old man to new man were accomplished, completed and tied up in a virtuous ribbon all of an evening. Such an impression would be false—in fact quite dangerous. Christian life is a process of growth and development in which we move into new phases of faith-life as we mature and respond more fully as persons to the love of Christ. As far as we are concerned, baptism in the Holy Spirit has been a decisive point, a major step on our spiritual exodus. Christ has changed our lives, shown us a depth of faith-life we had not known. We, by grace and not by ourselves, have responded more fully to him. But we are not suddenly perfect Christians or members of an elite clique of 'in' people. On the contrary we are very much on the road, in the process of becoming true Christians. We have a long way to travel it seems. It looks longer and harder now than it ever did before.

We have before us the task of being Christ in the world. That means that in, with, and through him, by the power of the Spirit we are to worship, love, and adore our Father, just as Jesus did. It also means that we, the corporate Body of Christ, must communicate the experience of the saving love of Jesus to the world. To the world means to mankind: not to men's feelings or emotions, not to men's disembodied spirits, but to human people in human societies and man-made institutions. The world that needs Jesus' love is shackled with poverty and disease, with racism and war, with lust for power and just plain indifference to the "other guy." This is the world we are sent to transform with Jesus' love, not so the world will be condemned but that it will be saved.

The two-pronged Christian life of worship and service in all the various forms it takes in today's Church is at the same time the most joyous and the most crucifying burden any man could assume. Yet that is what we must do, for we *are* Christ.

In this context it is clear that baptism in the Holy Spirit is not the end of Christian life; it is only the beginning. Some may call it a mountain-top experience—and indeed it is—but every one of us must come down the mountain with Jesus and walk to Jerusalem. We say this because there is a danger in pentecostalism, as in any good thing, to think once we have received it that we have really "arrived." From this arises the complacency that destroys the power of the Gospel. We have seen people receive a wonderful gift from God, in a renewal of the Holy Spirit and then do nothing with it. Perhaps they hold it up to the light and watch it glisten between their fingers. Or they display it prominently on the curio shelf, and then they grow cold, they atrophy, they do not use their gift or invest their talent, they grow no fruit—and the last state of that man is worse than the first. New life in the Spirit is given precisely to give new life, new activity, new motion. The gifts of the Spirit are tools of the body of Christ given to be used, fruits of the Spirit to be nurtured and grown. To receive the baptism in the Holy Spirit and then bask for a while in God's glory without responding to the daily call to worship and service, without walking in the Spirit, is very sad.

Yet to be lethargic is very easy. No one involved in the charismatic renewal has lost his share of freedom. At any moment we can and often do turn from the clear promptings of the Spirit. As in everything else, it is always easier to say No the second time, to be closed and indifferent. It may seem strange with the fantastic experience of the love and reality of Jesus being among us by the power of his Spirit that we should talk of coolness, rejection, and turning away. Yet is it so surprising? Think for a moment of how causally we can treat the eucharistic meal of the body and blood of Christ. Man has a remarkable capacity for losing his awareness of God, no matter what lengths God goes to abide with him.

Once in Texas, we heard a fine teacher, Robert Mumford, explaining the dynamic elements of the gifts and fruits of the Spirit. A certain man, he said, had been attending a regular class in gardening. One night he received some free gardening tools, a rake, a hoe, and a shovel. "Well," he thought, "I have certainly been blessed. I have the most beautiful tools." When he got home, he called to his wife and proudly showed her his rake, hoe, and shovel. She smiled warmly as she pictured the fruits of the new garden-to-be. In the morning his children stood admiring the tools gleaming in the kitchen corner—the rake, the hoe, and the shovel. Later the man hung them up in his garage and left the door open for all the neighbors to see. He thought himself quite the gardner and called in all his pals to look at his new tools.

They agreed that they were the finest rake, hoe and shovel ever seen. He left them hanging there and talked about them continuously, extolling their fine handles and sharp cutting edges. Whenever he got a chance he would witness to one and all about how he had been in need and had been given the most remarkable rake, hoe, and shovel. As they hung there they grew dusty and dull, then slightly rusty. And it was late summer, and there was no fruit.

To walk by the Spirit, to use the gifts, to build the Church, to preach the word: this is the charismatic life. This chapter is a practical discussion of walking in the Spirit. There is nothing particularly extraordinary here, just the sharing of our experience, our practices, concerns and difficulties. We have found the pentecostal communities around the country spontaneously developing certain guidelines for individual and community life in the Spirit. In the desire to share what may be helpful we present a number of practical suggestions.

How to Receive the Baptism in the Holy Spirit

The reality of the baptism in the Holy Spirit is offered by the Lord to all Christians who will accept it. As we said earlier, the baptism in the Holy Spirit, as we are using the term, is simply the radical reaffirmation of Christian initiation with expectant faith for the manifest workings of the Holy Spirit in our lives.

If the Lord is pouring out his Spirit on all who believe, then it seems that we need spend time only on this one point of belief. Put another way, what should be the faith and attitudes of those seeking the renewal in the Holy Spirit? Before praying for the baptism in the Holy Spirit the Christian should reflect upon his relationship with Jesus. We could discuss how a man becomes a believer in Christ, but that is really not the point. The question one can ask is: Do I personally realize and accept the saving love of Jesus for me? Do I genuinely respond to him in love? Do I know the Son of God as Lord? The answers to such questions should be obvious since they reflect a very basic choice in Christian life. The way these questions are worded may seem strange, but that is to help you to look at your faith from, perhaps, an unusual standpoint. As Catholics we have a tendency at times to get tied up in the details of our faith-life. The routine of religious observance can obscure what the observance is all about. Put bluntly, we should ask ourselves: Do I want to commit my life to Christ? Do I love him? This is a very here-and-now question, not meant to be an occasion for mulling over past mistakes. If you are at all uncomfortable with your relationship with Jesus, just make a simple affirmation of your faith here and now. Tell Christ in prayer that you believe in him and want to live in him. Actually it is good for all of us to renew this dedication of ourselves and then to act on it.

Often we meet friends and acquaintances who are on the fence about the matter of faith in Jesus. Observing the laws of Catholic life, they are not enjoying Catholic living because they are avoiding the central issue. We regularly suggest to the individual that he read one of the four gospels, right through from beginning to end. It should be read not as an historical document but with open receptivity as if the whole were speaking directly to the reader. This personal confrontation with the word of God will facilitate a mature commitment of faith.

Secondly, you must believe with lively faith what

the word of God teaches about the outpouring of .the Holy Spirit, Pentecost. The continuation of the life of Christ in the Church is the very heart of the Christian community in which every Christian is meant to share. The gifts and fruits of the Holy Spirit are really for the Body of Christ.

Further, you should acknowledge that you are already living in the Spirit through baptism, confirmation, holy eucharist and the other sacraments as well as through the life of prayer and action.

You must really believe that when we pray for a renewal in the Holy Spirit God will affirmatively answer that prayer. God puts very few conditions on our praying. One is that when we pray, we pray according to his will. We already know that it is his will for believers to be enlivened by the Holy Spirit, there is no question about that. A second is that we pray believing, with faith, with genuine expectation —not just in our minds but in our hearts and on our lips. Man is not a disembodied spirit. His faith, if it is to be personally his, must permeate his whole self: intellect, will, emotions, psyche, body. A man praying in real faith does not doubt when he prays, does not talk or think doubt; he speaks only his radical faith and trust in the Lord. Thus the person who asks God in faith, in the name of Jesus, to renew in him the outpouring of the Holy Spirit begun in baptism knows in faith that his prayer has been granted. It is as simple as that.

You must expect, accept and yield to the gifts of the Spirit at the moment of praying for baptism in the Spirit and in all the years that follow. It is here that people often have difficulty. It is helpful to remember that the gifts of the Spirit are revealed in the word of God and promised to the Christian people. Therefore to pray for them and expect them is not presumptuous. Secondly, the witness of millions of Christians throughout the world is a good indication that Jesus is pouring out the gifts of the Spirit in the Church today. It is happening now.

These points summarize the attitude of faith and expectancy one should have in praying for the baptism in the Holy Spirit. It seems clear that we will receive in proportion to our faith. While thinking about this step, it might be helpful to read the New Testament thoughtfully and prayerfully, to read other books on this subject or seek out Christians who have experienced the baptism in the Holy Spirit for advice and counsel. These practices can answer many questions and dispel lingering doubts. When all is said and done, it comes down to this: Do I really believe the risen Lord wants to share the fullness of his life with me?

What practical steps can be taken to receive the baptism in the Holy Spirit? A person certainly can seek out a nearby charismatic prayer group. Catholic and interfaith prayer groups exist all over the country and are becoming increasingly easy to find. Another possibility is to form your own prayer group with some friends. Perhaps you can study scripture together, read relevant materials and work out your questions as a group—all the while praying that the Lord will renew the life of the Spirit in you. Our friends in Pittsburgh prayed this way for several weeks; that's how the Catholic pentecostal movement began. One way or another, group prayer is **strongly** recommended just because of the communal nature of Christian life and the reality of Jesus where several are gathered together in his name.

If neither of these possibilities is open to you, direct prayer to the Father, in Jesus' name, is always open. Many people have received the baptism in the Holy Spirit in a moment of quiet, serious prayer. Alone with God they have prayed, and without a prayer group they have been convinced in their hearts of the depths of the reality of the Spirit of Jesus. They have begun to speak in other tongues as the Spirit gave them utterance. Prayer in faith for the baptism in the Holy Spirit can be made at any time in any place.

In any case, when the time comes and you are ready, you will pray with faith and you will receive. You need not work yourself up for anything nor feel anything, but only believe.

A good number of people experience a certain amount of natural fear at this point. Fear seems to be a preliminary to any authentic human love-response, fear of giving yourself completely, of losing yourself, of being out on a limb. We both recall that moment of fear when just before praying for the baptism in the Holy Spirit we were terrified by the proximity of God and the demands God might place on us. Why shouldn't we leave well enough alone, and maintain the comfortable, long-distance relationship we already had with Jesus? If he comes so close by the power of his Spirit, what is he going to do to me? This type of fear is normal; but Satan will attempt to exploit it, magnify it, and so to petrify your will.

God is love—love casts out fear. By God's grace we were able to overcome fear and to pray with ex-pectant faith. As we prayed, we knew more deeply and personally than ever before that the Lord, alive with us in the Spirit, loves us exceedingly. In that experience of love, all fear is banished; in that joy all burdens are sweet; in that peace all tasks for God are made light in the Spirit.

There is another kind of fear that can occur at this moment, depending on your temperament. If you are in a prayer group you may be inhibited by the others around you. You may fear they are looking at you, watching for the Spirit to manifest himself. In our experience such fear is not well grounded since everyone is deep in prayer, praising God for pouring out his Spirit on you. In a sense they are too busy to be watching for your reaction. However it will occasionally happen that something or someone might distract or disturb you. Should this happen, don't worry about it. We know a number of people who have prayed for a renewal in the Holy Spirit with a prayer group and because of some distraction have experienced absolutely nothing then and there. But when they got off by themselves they were met by the Holy Spirit. The prayer group may make a mistake, but the Holy Spirit will not. Trust him.

With your mind and will fixed only on what Jesus wants for you, believing what his word teaches us about his Spirit, expecting fully the gifts of his Spirit to be manifested in you, desiring the fruits of the Spirit to grow more abundantly in your life, with calm assurance ask the Lord Jesus Christ to renew your life in the Spirit and to pour out on you afresh this full share in his life.

"And I tell you, Ask, and it will be given you; seek, and you will find, knock, and it will be opened to you. For everyone who asks receives, and he who seeks finds, and to him who knocks it will be opened. What father among you, if his son asks for a fish, will instead of a fish give him a serpent; or if he asks for an egg, will give him a scorpion? If you, then who are evil, know how to give good gifts to your children, how much more will the heavenly Father give the Holy Spirit to those who ask him" (Lk. 11, 9-13).

How to Yield to the Gift of Tongues

Enough has been said about the nature of the gifts and fruits of the Holy Spirit that are consequences of receiving the baptism in the Holy Spirit. Praying in tongues is most often the first step in faith that a person wants to take. The origins and significance of this gift have already been discussed. Anyone honestly seeking baptism in the Holy Spirit is going to be open to all the gifts of the Spirit and to want to exercise them as the Lord gives them. The purpose and desirability of tongues is detailed by Saint Paul (in 1 Cor. 12-14). Here we want only to share our experience with this gift to help those who want to experience it.

The gift of tongues is not the baptism in the Holy Spirit. Rather it is a consequence, normally the first consequence, of receiving the baptism in the Holy Spirit. Some denominational Pentecostals hold that unless one speaks in tongues he has not received the Holy Spirit. This of course is entirely unacceptable for Catholic theology. We are praying for the gifts as manifestations of the Spirit already received.

However tongues must not be given short shrift. In the New Testament the gift of tongues is both a consequence of the outpouring of the Holy Spirit (Acts 2) which leads to tremendous spiritual growth, and it is an evidence of the fact that the Holy Spirit has been received (Acts 10). It is a sign to the individual and to the Church of the presence of the Spirit of Jesus, and it is cause for great celebration. From the day of Pentecost onward in Acts, speaking in tongues is a normal and usual result of the baptism in the Holy Spirit.

Today in the worldwide pentecostal movement, and among Catholics who have received the baptism in the Holy Spirit, praying in tongues is the normal and expected sign of the baptism in the Holy Spirit. It is usually, but not always, the first gift exercised. It is unquestionably a physical concretization of the presence of the Spirit. Once a person has yielded to the gift of tongues and given his body-person over so radically to the operation of the Spirit, the power and dynamic begin to flow tangibly and visibly through his life. It is the externalization of the interior work of the Spirit, and thus on the level of corporeality makes the experience of the Spirit real. It is the threshold to a life of walking in the power of the Holy Spirit. For all these reasons we must urge praying for and expecting the gift of tongues with the baptism in the Holy Spirit. From our experience we can say that the occasional man or woman who prays for the renewal in the Holy Spirit with grave mental reservations about tongues, or without being at least open to praying in tongues, may not be radically open to the workings of the Holy Spirit in his life.

However the vast majority of people who pray for baptism in the Holy Spirit are convinced of and desire the gift of tongues along with every other good thing the Lord wants them to have. Many people begin praising God in a new language right away.

But others have difficulty yielding to it. We use the word "yielding" deliberately. We are convinced that as far as the charismatic movement is concerned everyone touched by it is meant to pray in tongues, that in fact the gift of tongues is always given by the Lord as he renews the life of the Holy Spirit. The problem, if there is a problem, is in yielding to the gift that has been given. To us—Western, rationalistic, pragmatic people—tongues is a ridiculous gift. It is hard to "let go" and speak out in words we haven't thought through, carefully formulated and comprehended. To pray in tongues requires speaking out in an act of faith, words which are there but which are not known or understood.

Most Catholics face a further difficulty in that they are not accustomed to spontaneous vocal prayer, particularly in situations where others might hear them. Although raised in a tradition of quiet, prayerful onlooking at Mass, and of communal recitation of prayer formulas, we are now rapidly becoming used to uninhibited participation in the liturgy. The group dynamics involved in many renewal movements are also helping to free us from our former restraint. The realization that we are, in fact, the members of a Body, serving and helping each other, is increasing our openness to share our prayer life with each other. But the individual Catholic may still have considerable difficulty speaking out in English, much less in strange tongues. The following considerations may be helpful.

Praying in tongues is vocal prayer; that is, it is spoken aloud in an audible voice. That does not mean that praying in tongues has to be loud or even public at all. "For one who speaks in a tongue speaks not to men but to God" (1 Cor. 14, 2). Granted that on the natural level some people may pray in tongues in such a way that others can hear it, and that a prayer group expecting the sign of tongues received is glad to hear it—still, volume is a matter of personal choice. For some people it is good to pray in a raised voice. They need the assurance of hearing themselves praying in tongues. For others quiet prayer is more comfortable. Actually once a person begins to speak in tongues and is lost in prayer, the inhibitions disappear and the volume reaches a steady pitch without particularly attracting attention. About these matters there should be the greatest freedom.

When we pray in tongues we are doing the talking. In Acts 2, 4 we read "They were all filled with the Holy Spirit and began to speak in other tongues, as the Spirit gave them utterance." Speaking in tongues is not a passive reception, it is an active operation. On the physiological level it is your breath, your vocal cords, your lips and tongue which are working as they would in normal speech. But we know in faith that the sounds we hear, the language that comes forth, is of the Spirit. Even though it is meaningless to the human mind, its meaning is rooted in your faith, not in your natural understanding.

While praying for baptism in the Holy Spirit many people experience certain physiological signs that prompt them to speak out. For some the muscles of the throat constrict slightly, or the tongue begins to move spontaneously. If you have faith and respond to this urging by yielding your voice, you will have released the gift of tongues. For others, words or syllables are seen in the mind's eye or heard in the mind's ear. Speak out the syllables in faith. Still others have no such manifestations. One friend of ours, deep in prayer for the gift of tongues, decided to make a bodily act of faith, to give his voice to the Lord in trust. He spoke one syllable "Ah," that put the natural apparatus of speech in motion. Suddenly, without other mental images or promptings, he was praying in a new language, quite fluently and very conscious of the glory of the risen Lord.

It all comes down to this: All things are possible to him who believes. The gift is given. We need only respond by speaking out, not in English but in new words. Clearly we are doing the speaking, but the word of God tells us that the utterance is of the Spirit. The gift of tongues is received by faith.

Yielding to tongues takes some people a long time. It always remains strange and inexplicable, and we tend to get "hung up" on it. Then one day, perhaps suddenly, we find ourselves spontaneously praying in a new language. We both yielded to tongues a week after receiving the baptism in the Holy Spirit. Some have waited weeks and months before praying in tongues. This does not mean to imply that you should just wait passively for tongues. To speak in tongues is quite important, but it is far more important to seek the Spirit of Jesus. Those who do not yield to tongues immediately should not doubt that they have received the baptism in the Holy Spirit. Rather they should praise and thank God for all his gifts and start to walk in the Spirit using the various gifts and talents that have been given. In such a Spirit-filled life tongues will come if when we first prayed we really prayed in faith. Remember, neither tongues nor any other gift is to be sought for its own sake but rather for the building up of the Body of Christ, the glorification of Jesus, the worship of the Father and for the salvation of men.

A final word on receiving the baptism in the Holy Spirit and the gift of tongues to those who may find themselves in an ecumenical prayer group: One of the richest fruits of this contemporary charismatic movement is the binding together of Christians of many denominations in the Spirit of Jesus. Episcopalians, Lutherans, Presbyterians, Methodists, Baptists, Disciples, Nazarenes, Brethren, as well as denominational Pentecostals have become our very dear brothers and sisters in Christ, united by the baptism in the Holy Spirit. Christians from many of these denominations have similar backgrounds to ours in matters of liturgy, style and stance in prayer. However over the last seventy years a variety of different customs have grown up in some denominational pentecostal groups. Many of these fine Christians are convinced that their way of receiving the Holy Spirit, of receiving tongues, is the only way it can be done. Purely peripheral accretions and customs have become rigid rubrics for many Pentecostals. Very often these rubrics smack of frontier revivalism rather than of anything indigenous to the baptism in the Holy Spirit. If such a person is praying with you he may, in all good faith, instruct you in nonessentials such as raising your hands high, shaking your head vigorously, kneeling, or sitting, or yelling "glory halleluiah!" over and over. Sadly, we have observed the fraternal gesture of the "laying on of hands" turned into something of a rubdown. It must be made absolutely clear that such practices have essentially nothing to do with the baptism in the Holy Spirit. We must, of course, have mutual respect and be open enough to admit that in their own cultural contexts, where such practices are part of the warp and woof of popular liturgy, these customs can and do have real value. But to those of us from far different religious backgrounds, such actions imposed on a prayer group can impede the work of the Holy Spirit in our lives and prevent us from praying the prayer of faith. This should not be taken as a rejection of certain Pentecostal practices or a condemnation of any forms of worship. We have great respect for the customs and prayer style of our Pentecostal brethren. We freely join with them in this manner when meeting with them. But it is necessary to realize styles of praying are not an essential issue, that what is helpful to one man need not be helpful to all. Mutual respect must include mutual freedom on such issues. If you find yourself in this sort of situation, thoroughly distracted by differences in cultural forms, do not hesitate to request your Pentecostal brother simply to lay hands on you and pray quietly for your sake. Where there is true love and concern there will be no further problem.

Using the Gifts of the Spirit

We have already seen that the gifts of the Spirit operate in at least two different ways: in the context of a celebrating community gathered together to worship the Father and in the apostolic activity of the group or individual Christian. The fact that these gifts are to be exercised by members of Christ's Body means that we must cooperate with the Holy Spirit if they are to be operative at all. It is tremendously sobering to realize that the effectiveness of the Holy Spirit is limited by and depends upon the degree of openness and availability among the Christian people.

To exercise the gifts of the Spirit requires on our part an openness, an expectancy, and an active type of faith. Openness to the gifts of the Spirit is something that grows in a person as he experiences their operation with ever increasing familiarity. Although the gifts of the Spirit, particularly the more dramatic ones, were a bit startling to us at first, they became more acceptable and normal to us as we saw them in operation, bearing good fruit. Without being gullible we became increasingly aware of them as part of the normal experience of the charismatic community. Their occurrence became more the occasion for calm praise than for shocked astonishment.

With the experience of them, it becomes clear that the Christians exercising them are not possessed of "strange powers" nor are they mystic hermits surrounded by veils of clouds. They are, like all of us, just ordinary members of Christ's Body. This makes it obvious that healing, prophecy, discernment, knowledge, etc., are not so much the accomplishments of individual Christians as they are the accomplishments of Christ working by the power of his Spirit through the members of his Body. While it may be true that this man has a definite healing ministry, and is called a healer, or that woman who utters many prophecies is called a prophet, it is still more fundamentally correct to speak of these gifts as ministries of Jesus himself exercised by members of his Church. Through the Body, it is Christ who heals, it is the Spirit of Jesus who speaks. Therefore the individual is, from a certain point of view, relatively unimportant, and should not be seen as "this highly blessed and powerful man of God." The Lord will use anyone who is

open to being used. Receiving the ministry gifts has
nothing to do with being a wonderful person.

Because we all know our own sinfulness and are
aware of our shortcomings, we may close ourselves
to receiving the gifts of the Holy Spirit. We may feel
unworthy. This is a very healthy feeling because we
are unworthy. We are unworthy of the ministry gifts,
we are unworthy of baptism and the eucharist, we are
unworthy of salvation and God's love. The fact is
that the Lord uses the unworthy, saves the unworthy,
loves the unworthy. Realizing that the gifts of the
Spirit are meant to be exercised by ordinary Christian
people can do a lot to open us to exercising them
ourselves.

Secondly our lives should be characterized by the
continual expectation of the gifts of the Spirit, not
only those listed in 1 Cor. 12 but all the other gifts in
the Church, including those which the People of God
are discovering day by day. Those who are walking in
the Spirit should expect the Lord to be continually
manifesting himself, working in and through the
Church with all the various gifts of the Spirit. Very
close to the whole experience of the charismatic renewal is the realization that the Lord is working by
his Spirit in a remarkable way today. We should
expect his gifts to be here: In confusion expect
prophecy; in doubt expect teaching; for the disturbed
expect discernment; for the sick, healing. We should
be sensitive to the persons and situations we encounter, aware of what the Spirit might want to do
through us. The Christian, walking in the Spirit,
confronting difficult situations, should not bemoan
difficulties, but should reflect on gifts in the experience
of the community and seek the will of Jesus as to

how and what spiritual gifts he should exercise in faith.

Finally, the exercise of the gifts of the Spirit requires active faith. We will never exercise a ministry gift or see it bear fruit until we first step out in faith and act on our belief, trusting the Lord.

We are fond of praying over a number of verses from Heb. 11 which stress the basic role of faith in any authentic activity of the People of God. By faith Noah stepped out and built the ark in spite of what his neighbors thought; by faith Abraham moved out of his homeland in response to the God who called him, his friends and relations probably wagging their heads sadly. Again by faith Abraham trusted God and prepared to sacrifice Isaac; by faith Moses led the Israelites out of Egypt and across the Red Sea. All the folk-heroes of the Old Testament lived, toiled, worshipped, and died by faith. Faith it seems is the basic condition, the specific designation of man's relationship with God. Everything we are as Christians is done in and through faith. Our name is faithful.

In this context faith appears as a radical trust in Jesus in spite of the circumstances. The life of faith often looks foolish in the eyes of the world. The cry of the prophet, the claim of the healer, the stance of the teacher made in faith, can look ridiculous in the face of the harsh circumstances of the world we live in. But the man of faith acts in the face of the world.

Christian preachers and theologians through the ages have commented on the gospel scene where Peter, seeking Jesus, walks on the water. The disciples, sailing on the lake, see standing off on the water the figure of the Lord. Peter, impetuously bold, speaks out: "Lord, if it is you, bid me to come to you over

the waters." Jesus bids him, "Come." Peter's relationship with Christ is at the very core of his existence.
He believes radically in him. With his eyes and heart
set steadfastly on his Lord, he steps out in faith so
that he can come closer to Jesus. The water holds.
Peter is walking on the water, not by his power but
by his faith.

But then Peter, the type of every Christian, becomes aware of the "realities of the situation." He
is distracted by the circumstances which cry out that
his faith is absurd. Distracted, he takes his eyes off the
Lord, his faith wavers, and he begins to sink. The
Lord comes to him and holds him fast.

This is very much the situation of Christian faith
in action, a situation we have all experienced at some
time. Inasmuch as we take our eyes off the goal of
living only in Christ and declare that we can live only
in our own power, so much we fail. The faith that
yields walking on the water, the faith that enables us
to be fools for Christ and to step out into absurdity,
this is the condition of the person who would really be
used of God. It is itself a gift of the Spirit, often called
wonder-working confidence. Like all the other gifts, it
is taken by faith, but it grows in the test. It is the
catalyst for the exercise of the other spiritual gifts.
It is only by stepping out in this faith that we experience and communicate the power of the Holy Spirit.

The principle is well attested in scripture that
when we have faith—not just in our minds, but in our
hearts so that we lay it on the line in concrete action
—the ministry-gifts are successful. The ten lepers are
told by Jesus to go show themselves to the priest to
be declared cured. Still covered with disease, they
believe him and start out on the road to go to the

priests. The word says that as they went they were healed. The blind man on the road to Jericho, his eyes covered with mud, is told by Jesus to go to the pool and wash. He believes Jesus' word and lays his belief on the line. He acts and he sees. Faith in action yields the fruit of the gifts of the Spirit.

The charism of prophecy will never benefit the Church unless the prophet speaks out the phrase burning in his mind, trusting the Lord to complete his message. The man of discernment will never help build up the Body unless he has the courage to approach the one he discerns and speak in love. The gift of healing, the annihilation of suffering will not be shared unless we get out on that limb and pray with confidence for the sick. This is true both in a prayer meeting and in outside apostolic work, in the experience of day-to-day living.

The Prayer Meeting

The questions of when and how often to hold community prayer meetings cannot be answered univocally. The size of the group, its particular needs, the various types of people participating—these are some of the factors which must be taken into consideration.

If a charismatic prayer group is besieged for information and assistance by large numbers of people, it may be necessary to hold frequent meetings of an introductory character. If an established group draws Christians from all over a city, once a week or twice a month may be the occasion for a meeting several hours in length. But if the group is together in a college dorm, two half-hour periods in the week may be just right for them. Should the group be within a monastery or convent where the community spends hours a week in common prayer already, then a different form of meeting should be developed, perhaps religious meeting in two's and three's when it fits their schedule. In regions or states where there is a heavy concentration of groups in many cities and towns, a monthly day of renewal where all the groups come together on a Sunday in a central location has been very successful. At times we have held two types of meetings, one for the regular group where the emphasis is on prayer, and one for newcomers where the emphasis is on explanation and instruction. As a rule the people involved can best decide how and how often to meet.

If there is any structured format to the prayer meeting, it is indicated in Saint Paul: "When you come together, each one has a hymn, a lesson, a revelation, a tongue or an interpretation. Let all things be done for edification. If any speak in a tongue, let there be only two or three, and each in turn, and let one interpret. But if there is no one to interpret, let each of them keep silence in church and speak to himself and to God. Let two or three prophets speak, and let the others weigh what is said. If a revelation is made to another sitting by, let the first be silent. For you can all prophesy one by one, so that all may learn and all be encouraged; and the spirits of the prophets are subject to prophets. For God is not a God of confusion but of peace" (1 Cor. 14, 26-33). It seems to the exegetes that Paul is talking about the conduct of a meeting of the whole Christian community with something of an official character, perhaps even a eucharistic service. Even so, his guidelines serve very well for an "unofficial" gathering of contemporary pentecostals.

Translating this into our present situation we find that everyone wants to and is meant to contribute to the meeting—to lead a hymn, to share an insight into Christian living, to tell a story, to pray spontaneously, to prophesy, to exhort, to interpret tongues. In all of this there is great freedom and no pressure, with no particular sequence of events. The only rule of the house is that there be order and everyone speak in turn. This is rarely a difficulty in a community of love. In regard to interpretation, the combined experience of the group will answer that problem. If interpretation is regularly given, then it seems right for the man prompted to speak out to the group and yield to the Spirit, trusting the Lord for the interpretation. It should also be pointed out that a regular feature of prayer meetings is reading from the scriptures. Often this is planned in advance, often it occurs spontaneously. One thing Saint Paul does not mention explicitly is that meetings such as this enjoy periods of silence as well as periods of communal prayer.

All in all the meeting is a time of free sharing, of ministry to each other, of using the gifts of the Spirit to build up the Body of Christ, of seeing in faith the things we need from God; and all of this is carried on primarily in the atmosphere of praise. "Praise the Lord" is more than a slogan, it is the heart of the activity of the prayer group.

One spontaneous development, wherever prayer groups form, is the reception of the gift of leadership. Communities usually have their senior members, and prayer meetings usually have a leader or chairman.

Perhaps one man may regularly lead, or perhaps the function will rotate within the group. The leadership is actualized more in service than in authoritarian control. The leader is concerned with such weighty pastoral issues as "Are there enough chairs? Is it too hot in here? Did you remember to bring the coffee pot? O.k., let's start now." Within the meeting it is his concern to see that all things are done decently and in order, to bring the group back to prayer no matter how good the discussion gets, and to be extremely sensitive to the needs of others and to the operation of the Spirit.

As a prayer group develops more and more into a stable (though never closed) community, these Christians united in the baptism in the Holy Spirit, will experience both the joys and the difficulties of community life. This has reference not only to the conduct of the prayer meeting but to the lives of the members in the larger religious and social communities. Among the characteristics that have at times developed are:

(1) A desire, quite natural under the circumstances, to celebrate the eucharist together. There have been occasions when it has been possible to participate in the Mass at the conclusion of, or in close proximity to a prayer meeting. As experimentation with liturgical forms expands, the liturgists among us see great possibilities for the future integration of charismatic prayer meetings with the eucharistic assembly.

(2) A deep personal concern for each other and the growth of friendship in Christ. This leads not only to a broader social life with each other, but to the openness to share material property, food, money,

clothing. This is the development of a type of common life.

(3) The acceptance of fraternal correction in love. Leaders of communities are sensitive to the totality of the lives of their brothers and sisters. A person who unwittingly oversteps the bounds of decency and order in a prayer meeting is privately shown the better way. A person who is not living up to his civic or personal responsibilities is offered advice and counsel. Occasionally, very rarely in fact, a person who is incapable of community discipline, closed to the love of others, or unwilling to give of himself will join a prayer group. He can be quite sure that he is right and everybody else is wrong. This is a serious test of the love of Christ in a group. In our experience helping this type of person to open to the genuine operation of the Holy Spirit in the community may require serious fasting and prayer.

The preceding remarks are meant as help to those of you who will find yourselves leading prayer groups in the future. The leaders, elders, or senior members of any community receive from the Lord the gift and the duty of being more concerned about the inner life of the group. They must be sensitive to and aware of the various needs that arise.

But the area in which the role of leadership is most crucial is that of praying with people that they might receive the baptism in the Holy Spirit.

(1) The primary concern of the leader and the whole group is for the individual with whom they are going to pray. Are all the preliminary needs, questions and desires of this person met?

(2) We must remember that it is the Lord Jesus

who baptizes with the Holy Spirit and who renews the Holy Spirit, not the prayer group. At any time when the individual seeks it he will be met by the Lord.

(3) Therefore the responsibility of the leader or senior members is to prepare the individual by thoroughly explaining the baptism in the Holy Spirit, the gifts and the fruits of the Holy Spirit, including how to receive the gift of tongues. Care must be taken that the individual is satisfied and wants to go ahead. It is not necessary that this all be done in one night. The newcomer after receiving instruction should feel free to stop at that point, to spend some days or weeks praying the matter over, reading relevant material, talking with other people. When he is ready, the Lord will renew in him the life of the Holy Spirit. Our task is to help him get ready. This point of adequate preparation cannot be stressed too strongly. It makes no sense to rush a man to encounter God before he is capable of fully responding in faith.

(4) Praying with an individual or group of people for the baptism in the Holy Spirit should not usually be part of the public prayer meeting but should be done probably in another room or after a break in the meeting. Those present should include several people to lay on hands, pray, and counsel. Spectators, curious onlookers, however well intentioned, are to be asked to leave. This has nothing to do with secrecy but rather with the privacy fitting such a personal encounter with the Lord Jesus, the personal comfort of those being prayed for, and the great value in solidarity in expectant faith of everyone present.

(5) The leaders should have already appointed

several people to lay hands on those asking prayer and several others to remain in prayer and counsel with them after the laying on of hands. It must be remembered that for the individuals involved this is a moment of intense prayer which is made concrete here and now by the imposition of hands. For that reason those ministering in this way should proceed as a group to each person individually and in order. Experience has taught us that there is nothing more confusing at this time than a number of individuals milling about laying on hands helter skelter. Nothing is more beautiful than the fraternal love that leads us to pray for one another, but it must be carried out in an orderly manner and under the authority of the leadership in the prayer group. The gifts of the Spirit must work together if the Church is to be built up.

(6) When everyone is ready the leader should begin with prayer praising and thanking the Lord for the gift of his Spirit, reminding all of Christ's real presence in their midst. As the individual ministry begins, we have found it helpful to pray over each person a prayer commanding Satan and all evil spirits to depart from the individual in Jesus' name and to return to hell. The explicit rejection of the devil in Jesus' name, done in faith, is a helpful preparation to receiving the gifts and fruits of the Holy Spirit. This is followed by an explicit invocation of the Holy Spirit and the laying on of hands.

(7) Often with this gesture or in the counsel and prayer immediately following, the gifts of the Spirit begin to be manifested. It is in this period that those newly renewed in the Spirit should have continual fellowship in prayer and gladness with other Chris-

tians. Leaders and counselors should be prepared to spend a good deal of time then and in succeeding days with the new members of the community.

But when all these practical details have been attended to, when everyone has a prayer meeting to go to and a way to get there, and when the regular prayer meeting is an established part of the community life, one thing must remain absolutely clear: The purpose of the baptism in the Holy Spirit is not to create prayer groups or to spread the practice of prayer meetings. The prayer meeting up to now has been a useful structure for our Christian lives. It is only a tool, it is not our goal. The purpose of baptism in the Holy Spirit is the renewal of persons, of structures, of institutions, of the Church by bringing about the realization of the risen Lord and the present power of his Spirit for true worship and effective apostolic work. For some this may mean regular prayer meetings, for others occasional prayer meetings but a more radical life of involvement in the concerns of society. The gifts of the Spirit are not operative only in prayer groups. They operate wherever the Spirit-filled Christian confronts the world with the word of life.

Nurturing the Fruits of the Spirit

Later we will discuss the growth of the spiritual life in relationship to and within the public activity of the Church, the life of liturgy and renewal. But for a person to enter fully into such projects there is a need for an accompanying program of spiritual development. It is not in the prayer meetings but in our private lives, relationships, and occupations that the authenticity of the fruits of the Spirit is to be manifested.

There is a key to the nurture of these fruits, as you might expect, similar to the gifts. The fruits should be expected in difficult situations. Their first signs or impulses should be yielded to and celebrated. In distress claim peace; in hate-filled situations claim love; in deep sadness, profound joy; in trial, long-suffering. While it is true that the fruits of the Spirit grow in the actuality of interpersonal relationships, still they are grounded in the quality of our interpersonal relationship with Jesus. It is in our conversation with him, our simple personal discursive prayer, that the fruits of the Spirit are nourished.

Fundamental to this whole process is our use of the word of God. One of the most universally experienced consequences of the baptism in the Holy Spirit is the spontaneous turning to the word of God. Even for those who have never read the bible before, it becomes a mainstay of their spiritual lives and the source of much growth. Inasmuch as we are faithful to scripture as the heart and foundation of our spiritual reading and study, the fruits of the Spirit will grow within us.

In the joyful, prayerful reading of the word of God we are not merely learning of our religious heritage, of the wonderful works of God throughout salvation history, but God by his Spirit speaks to us; he communicates his life-giving word to us. When we read scripture we are praying by listening to what the Lord has to say to us. Then when we pray ourselves we can respond to his word in praise, in thanksgiving and in intercession.

In this way the Lord teaches us, guides us, and

shows us his will. Our response to renewal in the
Holy Spirit will be so much more fruitful if it is
centered on God's word.

Our response to God's word can take many forms,
and once again we come into an area of personal
taste and freedom. All of us in the charismatic movement have shared a new facility in conversational
prayer. Conscious of the presence of Jesus in our
lives, in our homes, in this room, we talk freely and
spontaneously to him. This is not talking to yourself,
not the introspective mulling over of who I am, but
talking to Jesus present to me by the power of the
Spirit. It may be strange at first, like meeting an old
friend on a new, a deeper level of relationship, but
it grows easy, warm and genuine.

At other times we may use the formulas of prayer
so precious in our tradition: the psalms, the little
offices, the rosary. Different people are expected to
have different likes and dislikes in this area. What
is important is that all of us develop and nurture
our own style of personal prayer and be faithful to
it. As you grow in prayer, in sensitivity to God, you
find God speaking to you through everything you
encounter.

Just as the word of God is the wellspring of our
prayer response, so also it is the basis of our study.
We must never minimize the importance of "continuing education" in the Christian life. One of the
greatest tools of darkness against the light of the
Gospel is ignorance. Ignorance divides, confuses,
hinders, and turns off the plan of redemption. We are
intellectual beings, and we communicate the saving
love of Jesus as much with our intelligent understanding as with any other human faculty. In an age of

fast-moving reform and change within the Church there is no excuse for remaining uninformed. The Christian must be a person of study whatever his level of educational development. The word of God, the teaching and history of the Church, the importance of the Second Vatican Council, the tasks of the liturgical and ecumenical movements, and the relationship of all the social, political and economic revolutions to the Gospel of Jesus Christ—these must be our daily intellectual fare. No day should go by in the life of the Christian who would serve his Lord that some time is not spent reading and understanding in these areas.

The fruits of the Spirit ultimately grow and take root throughout the structure of the Church and the world as we put them into action. Our prayer and our study, both anchored in the word of God, enable us to manifest the word. We must recall that we are gathered together not just as a worshipping assembly but that we are sent out as Jesus was sent.

We do not have to search for fields in which the fruits of the Spirit must be planted. How quickly the structures of renewal spring up around us, how thirsty they are for living water. It seems to us that our task is not to create a "pentecostal structure" in the Church, but to bring the renewal of Pentecost to the existing and arising organisms of concern.

The layman is on the move. Yes, thank God, after centuries of watching the Church, he has realized that he is the Church. So he is taking upon his own shoulders tremendous responsibilities in terms of the governance, fiscal management, education, and the apostolate of the Church. He sees himself sharing an equally important if different function than the hierarchy. He is determined to fully actualize his membership in the Body of Christ. Such a movement is not without tension. Crises of education and communication lead to crises of authority which send shudders through the worldwide structure of the Church.

Come, holy Spirit, and from heaven direct
on man the rays of your light.

Throughout the Church there are cries for radical reform in the training function and style of life of clergy and religious. Restoration of the values of primitive monasticism parallels the drive for optional celibacy for secular priests. Some would have the priesthood more wrapped up in the concerns of the world. Others demand that the whole Church, from the Vatican to the parish level, strip itself of its enormous wealth, give what it has to the world's poor and live in evangelical poverty. Whole communities of religious are abandoning their canonical status only to regroup as private communities of unofficial nuns or brothers to better preach the Gospel. Yet there are other voices, strong voices, which cry out that the old order must be preserved for the glory of God.

Come, father of the poor; come, giver of God's
gifts, come, light of men's hearts.

Contemporary theology, coupled with mass media of communication, is continually reexamining and restating the truth of Christianity. The latest thinking is no further away than the bookstore, and hundreds of thousands of educated Catholics are reading, thinking, and evaluating the traditional teaching of the Church. New *credos* follow on the heels of new catechisms, as intellectually conservative and progressive elements in the Church vie for the allegiance of the faithful. Some bemoan the confusion, others rejoice in the creativity of healthy tension and dialogue.

Kindly Paraclete, in your gracious visits to man's soul you bring relief and consolation . . .

The Catholic bishops of the world meet in Rome, the leaders of the World Council of Churches assemble in Uppsala, while the World Federation of Evangelicals has its own meeting. Each one cries out, "One Lord, one faith, one baptism." Each one calls for genuine ecumenism. But what does each one mean? How are we to be one in the Spirit, what agreement is there among us at all? Are we rushing into fellowship without common faith? Shall we have any criteria for unity? What is the role of the Catholic Church in fulfilling Christ's prayer that we all might be one? Must we change, accommodate, or maintain, the bulwark of orthodoxy?

If it is weary with toil, you bring it ease; in the heat of temptation, your grace cools it; if sorrowful, your words console it.

War in Vietnam. Catholics on picket lines in protest. Catholics on chow lines in training camps. Catholics in prison for their convictions. Catholics in trenches for their convictions. The Students for a

Democratic Society and the Young Americans for Freedom both have within their ranks committed, dedicated young Christians convinced of the truth of their positions and programs. On this issue alone what tension, what hatred among brothers and sisters, fathers and sons. What in the name of God is the Christian's role in terms of applied force and violence in the face of evil in the world?

Light most blessed, shine on the hearts of
your faithful—even into their darkest corners;

The plight of the American Negro. Christians living in suburbia, whisking at rooftop level through ghettos on our freeways. The poor, the starving, the rat-infested minorities of our cities. Job training, more welfare, more beauracracy, upward bound, more looting, more sniping, guaranteed annual wage, guaranteed annual death. Sisters on picket lines in Milwaukee for open housing, Christians going to court to protect the value of their property. Canon Law Society picketed for meeting in a segregated club. What is our Christian duty? Is there a clear answer?

For without your aid man can do nothing good,
and everything is sinful.

Poverty in our nation and around the world. Starving millions. How to share our food, how to finance emerging nations? Bishop Sheen taxes his rich parishes for the poor. Protest. The Eucharistic Congress is held in Bogotá—hundreds of thousands of dollars for vestments, finery, for food and hotel bills in the heart of impoverished Latin America. Protest.

Barbara Ward calls for one percent of the Atlantic alliance's annual gross national product for the poor —she begs at the World Council of Churches in the name of Jesus. Inaction. Yet these same poor, emerging nations are seen by many of the faithful as the rise of an anti-Christian, pro-Communist wave of lawlessness and totalitarian violence. Many feel they must be stopped if Christianity and the Gospel message are to survive.

Wash clean the sinful soul, rain down your grace on the parched soul and heal the injured souls . . .

Catholics, always in politics, are scrambling for leadership in our national affairs. They go as Christians, as witnesses of Jesus as well as Americans before our people. They stand on every conceivable side of every issue. They work, they drive, they suffer, and they die. Liberals and conservatives, Democrats and Republicans, Northerners and Southerners. Increasingly the Catholic press, Catholic educators, clergy and laity alike, are rolling up their sleeves, jumping into the political arena, driven by their Christian convictions.

Soften the hard heart, cherish and warm the ice-cold heart, and give direction to the wayward.
Give your seven holy gifts to your faithful for their trust is in you.

There is no end to the issues and the positions in this age of renewal. Nor can we, nor anyone else among us, claim to share fully the mind of Christ on

these problems. But this we can know: We are his
Body, he is our head, and he is concerned. It seems
clear that a major contribution to the success of the
renewal of the Church—as demonstrated by the pain-
ful problems of internal change and the serious issues
of outside involvement—can be made by those who as
bearers of the fruits of the Holy Spirit do get thoroughly involved. The Holy Spirit comes and works
in the Church and fills and heals the problems of the
Church when we allow him to enter our midst, when
we bear him to the front lines so that his presence
infuses the Christian responses to the issues.

"Come Holy Spirit"—its plea and its claim will
never be accomplished in Christ's Church unless we,
no matter what our personal stands or convictions,
seek first to nourish the fruits of the Spirit by a life
of action.

> Give them heavenly reward for their combat
>   here below;
> Give them a death that ensures salvation;
> Give them unending bliss. Amen. Alleluia!

The Charismatic Life and the Liturgy

Walking in the Spirit, the gifts and fruits of the
Spirit, prayer meetings, renewing the baptism in the
Holy Spirit—all these are essentially grounded in the
liturgy. It is from the liturgy that they take their
origin. What is renewed in the pentecostal movement
is born in the waters of baptism, and is nourished in
the continual celebration of the death and resurrection of Christ as we gather at the altar. In itself the
worship of the Church embodies on the level of
human religious celebration the totality of the Christ-
event. Everything that Jesus Christ's redemptive love

has wrought is made continually present at Mass, in the sacraments, in the divine office of the People of God. Yet no one of us, no one community of us can apprehend or embody all of that reality. The paschal mystery is here among us, yet veiled in signs and rites it is not fully here. For we do not recall the death of the Lord only as so much purchase made, bought and paid for; we proclaim it until he comes and brings all to completion. The eschatological hope of the coming Lord in glory keeps us all on tiptoe, watching the signs of the times and quick to build the Kingdom.

The pentecostal movement flowing from the liturgy is not only radically incarnational but markedly eschatological. In it the risen Lord anointed is more fully present and active, more quickly coming to the eyes of faith. It is nothing which is not already celebrated in the official worship of the Church; it is but a deeper realization of this reality among the faithful. It is the actualization on the level of personal faith-in-action of the Christ-event we commemorate.

Thus there is no discord between the charismatic movement and the liturgy. There is perfect harmony. The overwhelming majority of Catholics who have received baptism in the Holy Spirit have been drawn more closely to the liturgical life of the Church as to the very source of life. There has been no tendency on the part of Catholic pentecostals to substitute prayer meetings or any of the gifts for the sacramental life of the Church. In fact the visibility of the prayer meeting as a type of freewheeling word service evokes a hunger for the fulfillment of the eucharistic meal. As the charismatic life flows from the liturgy, so it returns to the liturgy for completion.

Yet the pentecostal Catholic does not return to

celebrate the death and resurrection of Christ empty-handed. He comes to Mass full of faith, having seen for himself in the Spirit-filled life "that which was from the beginning, which we have heard, which we have seen with our eyes, which we have looked upon and touched with our hands" (1 Jn. 1, 1) — Jesus Christ alive and active among his people by the power of his Spirit. He comes with a deeper experience of Christian life, of the ministry gifts, of the here-and-now power of the Spirit. This new faith builds up the fruitfulness of the eucharistic celebration. As each of us comes to the table we bring everything the Lord has made of us as members of his Body. Gathered together to celebrate the death and resurrection of Jesus, Spirit-filled yet hungry, we give fuller praise and glory to the Father of the Lord.

Appendix I

(A.) An introduction to a Catholic pentecostal movement cannot be complete without some indications of the historical roots of pentecostalism itself and the existence of similar manifestations of the Spirit, whatever they may have been called, throughout the history of the Church. For that reason we append here the briefest outline of such developments, urging the reader to follow up through the bibliographic suggestions for a thorough study of the subject.

We have already remarked in one or two places that the New Testament Church made no radical distinction between institutional and charismatic elements in the community. On the contrary, as the Spirit of Jesus was seen to enliven every fiber of the body, so he was seen as the giver and indweller of every gift-office-ministry that was part of the Church. Saint Paul has left us four lists of examples of such gift-ministries of the Spirit (Rom. 12; twice in 1 Cor. 12; Eph. 4). It is perfectly clear from his teaching in 1 Cor. 12 and elsewhere that all these functions are of the one Spirit and that they must operate in conjunction and harmony with each other. The gift to be a bishop is as charismatic as the gift to be an interpreter of tongues. The task of run-of-the-mill administration is just as Spirit-filled as that of casting

249

out demons in Jesus' name, even though the latter is more dramatic. The New Testament model for church order does not indicate a hierarchical institution in healthy tension with a more freewheeling charismatic element.

On the other hand, as we have already indicated, a division of emphasis is discernible in the Church of the patristic era. The hierarchical gifts became increasingly institutionalized and became the official structure of the Church. Simultaneously the immediacy of their spiritual provenence was obscured. The whole notion of charismata was applied more and more to the dramatic, startling gifts, often experienced on the unofficial level of subjective faith-life, e.g. among the desert monks, hermits, secluded visionaries.

All efforts of reform and renewal in the Church have emphasized one or the other of these aspects of Church life, institutional or spiritual. Institutional reforms have had as their chief concern proper church order. Spiritual reforms stressed the authenticity of the life of faith. Among the former are reformers such as Gregory the Great, Charlemagne, Luther, Zwingli, and the Council of Trent. Among the latter are Francis of Assisi, Joachim of Floris, Ignatius Loyola, Francis DeSales, George Fox, John Wesley, Billy Graham, and Thomas Merton.

At their worst, institutional reforms, tending to be cold and legalistic in character, often fell short of their goals because they substituted politics for authentic piety. On the other hand, spiritual reforms often began to bear the fruit of the Spirit but then either grew cold through complacency, or drifted into spiritual extremes because they were not able to move forward in a friendly atmosphere with the hierarchy or with a vibrant sacramental life.

It is among these latter groups of spiritual reform that the more dramatic gifts of the Spirit were often manifested. Because such movements often existed with the mere tolerance or even open opposition of the institutional structure, they were branded "enthusiastic" or ultra-supernatural. The implication in such epithets is that such movements are dangerous because they tend to go beyond the normal means of grace and they expect more than the normal results and effects of grace. The flaw in such criticism is its failure to recognize the impoverished condition of the normal means and effects when they are circumscribed by a form of institutionalism that tends to quench the Spirit and lacks an emphasis on the role of personal experience for a truly authentic faith. It is a fact of history that spiritual reform movements have often been suppressed by the hierarchy as dangerous or forced out of the Church because they sprang up unofficially among the people rather than being handed down to the people from the hierarchy. When such movements were forced out of the Church then indeed many of them brought forth spiritual excesses, cut off as they were from the responsible guidance the hierarchy could have given them if the institution itself had been open to genuine spiritual reform.

Today however the dichotomy between institution and charism is being gradually healed over. There has never been such a time as this when the hierarchy is so actively promoting the growth of authentic spiritual values among the people. In the Second Vatican Council we have a remarkable instance of a reform council equally concerned about the authentic faith-life of persons and correct church order. In this prevailing atmosphere it is to be hoped that a movement such as charismatic renewal will be able to exist fruitfully within the institutional structure while at the same time serving and contributing to the renewal of the Church.

(B.) The modern pentecostal movement is about seventy years old. Until 1967 the experience of baptism in the Holy Spirit followed by the gifts and fruits of the Spirit, recognized as such and organized along such lines, did not exist in the American Catholic Church. The vast majority of the two million pentecostal Christians in the United States either belong to one of the pentecostal denominations, or have remained within their denomination of origin. Until about 1956 the movement was religiously and culturally confined, although not absolutely, to Protestants of an evangelical or fundamentalist background. Since 1956 there has been a rapid growth of pentecostalism among Protestants from denominations belonging to the World Council of Churches. This latter development is called neo-pentecostalism.

If we set out to uncover the historical roots of pentecostalism in modern times, we could begin with the more evangelical and spiritualistic elements of the Protestant Reformation, or at least with certain seventeenth and eighteenth century developments, especially in England and Germany. Putting other issues to one side, one of the major contributions of the sixteenth century Reformation was its reemphasis on the subjective aspect of faith-life in which the believer comes to know the Lord on a personal level. It is chiefly on the basis of knowing Jesus or knowing him in a deeper way that the reform movements proceded among magisterial Protestants who emphasized the authenticity of faith-life.

In seventeenth century England there arose the Society of Friends, or Quakers, mainly under the leadership of George Fox. A highly spiritualistic movement with little liturgy or form, the Friends stressed deep personal union with Christ through obedience to the Inner Light which every human being has within him and to which he is to be sensitive. The ministry of George Fox and his close associates was accompanied by visions, discernment, healing, and to some degree tongues.

In the later eighteenth century the Methodist revival began in England with John Wesley. Wesley, an Oxford don and priest of the Church of England was thoroughly taken with the realization of the saving love of Christ for the individual. This assurance and the achieving of holiness and sanctification on the basis of this assurance became the center of Wesley's preaching. For many decades he travelled the length and breadth of the British Isles, to the Continent and to America, bringing hundreds of thousands of Church members to a deep personal conversion. Those who followed him were organized into small classes and societies which followed certain techniques of spiritual discipline—their "method," from which the name Methodists. This revival movement intended to stay within the Church of England and to renew it spiritually; however schism did develop. Wesley's ministry involved not only traditional practices but innovations such as the society meetings and open air preaching. His ministry also was marked by "enthusiastic outbursts," including healing and tongues.

Contemporary with Methodism, similar yet different, was the Moravian Brethren movement in Saxony under the leadership of Count Zinzendorf. Once again we find a highly evangelical movement directed toward personal faith life and meant to enliven the Lutheran state Church from within. This movement, too, developed into a new denomination.

When we turn to the situation in America, we find no universal establishment of any denomination and that denominationalism is the order of the day. The chief characteristic of American Christianity is its voluntarism—"go to the church of your choice." At the beginning of our national existence Catholics were a small minority. The Protestant churches—Episcopalian, Congregationalist, Presbyterian, Baptist, with an increasing influx of Lutherans, Methodists, and small but concentrated Quaker-Brethren-Mennonite groups—all shared in common the basic Reformation emphasis on personal experience of Christ the Lord and mature conversion from a life of sin to a life of grace. At the end of the eighteenth century, these groups cooperated to some degree in launching a broad program of evangelistic revivalism in the United States. This inter-denominational cooperation continued throughout most of the nineteenth century, although increasing differences in emphasis and teaching often limited the number of denominations cooperating in a given revival.

American revivalism with its emphasis on personal conversion, often called the crisis experience of salvation, was a mainstay of nineteenth century American

life, particularly on the expanding frontier. The
itinerant evangelist with the support of local ministers
would come into an area, set up his tent and begin to
preach the Gospel. At the end of each meeting sinners
would be invited to come forward and accept Christ
as their personal Lord and Savior. This type of
evangelism was accompanied by hymn singing, loud
praying, shouting and hand clapping. It had its share
of miracles, healings, casting out of demons and
tongues. Often a carnival atmosphere prevailed which
was fertile ground for emotional excess. Because of the
educational level of both clergy and people the revivals were often characterized by inadequately simplistic catechesis and theology.

One type of revival movement, called Campbellite,
stressed the word of God well enough, but the word
as understood and interpreted by "good common
sense." From this somewhat more rationalistic revival
emerged the Disciples of Christ in the north and the
Christian Church in the south as new denominations.
Baptist revivals stressing the totality of one conversion
experience spread in the south and west and Baptist
congregations flourished in great numbers. Another
type of revival was held by the Holiness Movement
which grew from early Methodism's emphasis on
personal holiness. In distinction to the Baptist concept
of one experience of grace, the Holiness Movement
held for two experiences of grace, one for conversion
or salvation, the second for complete holiness or
sanctification. Sometimes this second experience was
referred to as a Holy Ghost baptism, or Spirit baptism.
On the other hand Baptists tended to connect the
phrase baptism in the Holy Ghost with the simple
crisis experience of conversion. Thus the idea of a

baptism in the Holy Spirit of some sort was known in late nineteenth century revival circles.

The Holiness Movement separated from Methodism toward the end of the nineteenth century. Its denominations include the Church of the Nazarene, the Church of God, and smaller denominations with the word "holiness" in their name.

In 1900 Bethel Bible School was opened in a simple house in Topeka, Kansas. There were about nine students gathered there to study the word. Typically, the bible was their only textbook. As far as we can tell, most of the people there were from a Holiness background. The subject of their study centered on the idea of the baptism in the Holy Spirit. They came to the conclusion that the only sure and scriptual sign of the baptism in the Holy Spirit was speaking in tongues. On January 1, 1901 a woman student was in prayer during the evening. She experienced the peace and joy of Christ and began to praise God in tongues. Within a few days the whole community had received the baptism in the Holy Spirit in this way and the modern pentecostal movement was born.

This experience accompanied by strong ministries of conversion, healing, prophecy, etc., spread to Texas and (in 1906) to Los Angeles where it grew substantially, thence to Chicago, New York, London, and Scandinavia by 1915.

The experience of baptism in the Holy Spirit followed by tongues and other ministry gifts was regularly rejected by most baptistic and holiness congregations. The new pentecostals found themselves excommunicated from their own churches, and they spontaneously formed their own assemblies. By 1914 American pentecostals were so numerous that some form of national organization was necessary. The Assemblies of God was incorporated in that year, and to this day it is the largest pentecostal denomination in this country. However there have been many other pentecostal denominations formed, numbering now about thirty-five, divided regionally, culturally, racially and doctrinally.

About denominational pentecostalism we make two remarks of special interest to Catholics: (1) The pentecostal denominations surrounded the essentially valid experience of the baptism in the Holy Spirit with the religious style, culture, worship and theology of American revivalism because it was in that context that the baptism in the Holy Spirit was experienced. They simply carried their religious traditions with them. However it should be clear that these elements are not essential to the baptism in the Holy Spirit. (2) The baptism in the Holy Spirit with its gifts and the fruits, particularly the gift of tongues, became the *de facto* heart of Christianity, the center of life in Christ for denominational pentecostalism. This tended to exclude other valid and necessary elements for full Christian life. Obviously this has not happened with Catholic pentecostalism, where the experience of the baptism in the Holy Spirit has been integrated into the totality of the life of the Church.

Since 1900 pentecostalism has been the fastest growing form of Christianity in the world. Today there are 10,000,000 pentecostals world wide, two million in the United States. Since 1956, as we said above, the charismatic life has been growing by leaps and bounds among Episcopalians, Lutherans, Presbyterians and Methodists. By and large, those experiencing this newer dimension of faith life have remained in and contributed to the well-being of their own denominations. In the same way, but with a somewhat spontaneous origin, the charismatic renewal has now appeared in the Catholic Church in America.

This is just the briefest summary of the antecedents, origin, and growth of pentecostalism. A thorough study of spiritual movements within Christianity throughout the centuries and of pentecostalism in particular should be of considerable assistance in pointing to consistently desirable elements and in avoiding Spirit-quenching mistakes.

Appendix II

It is obvious to the reader at the conclusion of this book that it was not conceived or written as a definitive theological treatise. While it is essential to our purpose that the theological analysis of pentecostalism presented here be basically correct and adequate, this book was written for an audience more broadly based than the theologically expert. Our concern has been to tell the story accurately and to explain it sufficiently to benefit the Catholic community at large. Furthermore, the brief time span of the Catholic pentecostal movement to date has not permitted sufficient reflection for a thorough theological analysis of charismatic renewal. In the area of theology, if we have made any contribution, it has been merely to break the ice.

If the pentecostal movement grows among Catholics with any of the alacrity with which it has spread in the overall Protestant world, a continuing effort to reflect on the experience and its meaning for the total Church will be demanded of theologians. A number of competent Catholic theologians with markedly different points of view are already personally involved in the movement. If theology can be described as an intellectual reflection upon and examination of an experience of faith-life, then it is to be expected that these men and women, the "pentecostal theologians," will be called upon to work in this direction.

On the other hand, since pentecostalism claims to be for the whole Church today, it seems necessary to call for serious theological analysis by theologians of all standpoints within the whole Church who are uncommitted to and unconvinced of pentecostalism's value. It is our hope that the present book will serve as a springboard for all types of contemporary theological investigations. We do not mean to imply that this book lacks value on the theological level. While popular in presentation, our explanation is still the fruit of extensive study, especially in the areas of scriptural exegesis, liturgiology, and sacramental theology. The whole, however, has been purposely presented in the framework of traditional biblical and catechetical thought categories. To speak of sin and grace, heaven and hell, God and Satan, supernatural and natural, is to speak in the commonly intelligible vocabulary of Christian tradition. This is the language of the word, of the liturgy, of the Fathers, of the magisterium, and of contemporary middle-of-the-road to right-wing theologization. It is a language not only suitable to communicate with the largest number of people, but it is also to serve as an adequate and faithful expression of our experience which we know to be a reality. On the other hand, foreseeing objections arising from the theological left, it should be made quite clear that such language is much more the vocabulary of our faith-life than an enunciation of principles for a universal cosmology.

Contemporary systematic theology is engrossed with the question of natural vs. supernatural—or better yet, supernature as the core of nature. The radical dichotomy between heaven and hell assumes more clearly the role of meaningful religious symbol as the three-storied universe of the ancient world confronts not only the Copernican revolution but the double-barreled *coup de grace* of modern physics and depth psychology. Thus some persons develop new categories of religious expression radically incarnated in the philosophical-psychological experience of North American and West European intellectual life, while others maintain the value, meaning, and even richer meaning of traditional categories of faith-expression precisely in the confrontation with absurdity and the meaninglessness of "modern man." Surely, then, the values of pentecostalism as a meaningful and valid part of Christianity can be approached from both the theological left and right. It seems that those theologians who operate from the canons of the social sciences of psychology, sociology, and anthropology have much to contribute to a deeper understanding of pentecostalism. This is true not only in regard to the vertical aspect of the worship of God but especially in regard to the horizontal aspect of pragmatic, effective, and successful integration of personalities in community in a secular world.

It should be obvious that we have not adopted the methodology of fundamentalism. Too often in the past Christians experiencing baptism in the Holy Spirit have adopted not only the cultural environment of denominational pentecostalism but also the thought categories of the fundamentalist milieu. We do not mean to criticize fundamentalism in itself. It forms the theological mind-set of millions of excellent Christians and has played an important role in building the Body of Christ in many cultures. Secondly, where fundamentalist Christianity has dried up into dead dogmatism, pentecostal fundamentalism has been a great service in reviving genuine, living, and dynamic Christianity. Our approach has been more rooted in the ongoing evolution of Christian life. We have, however, been unreservedly kerygmatic in our approach, convinced that the proclamation of the fullness of the Good News will speak to the hearts of men and bear good fruit in the Body of Christ. It is this existential, concrete, handing on of a living faith experience which gives rich and lasting meaning to persons in the world, which contemporary theology, both right and left, must recognize as the *de facto* reality of the pentecostal movement. It must be recognized that theological investigation not only from the traditional *loci* but also from the modern social sciences can add much to our understanding of pentecostalism, help to free it from the peripheral cultural forms which can become idolatrous concerns, and gather from it broad implications for the life of the Church. It is our hope that such investigations can go forward, if not in a totally unbiased way, then at least in an open way; and that with the publication of this book such theologization will have an adequate foundation to build on.

Suggested Reading

1. STIRRINGS IN PITTSBURGH

Mary Papa, "People Having a Good Time Praying," *The National Catholic Reporter,* vol. 3, no. 29 (May 17, 1967). Quotations from this eyewitness article introduce each chapter.

John Sherrill, *They Speak With Other Tongues,* New York: Spire, 1965.

David Wilkerson, *The Cross and the Switchblade,* Westwood, N. J.: Spire, 1964.

3. ROOTS OF THE BAPTISM IN THE HOLY SPIRIT

W. M. Abbott, *The Documents of Vatican II,* New York: America Press, 1966. This is the source for all quotations from the Council cited in this book.

R. Beraudy, "L'Initiation Chretienne," *L'Eglise en Priere: Introduction a la Liturgie,* ed. A. G. Martimort, Paris: Desclee, 1965, pp. 528–584.

Jean Chrysostom, *Huit catecheses baptismales,* ed. A. Wenger, Sources Chretiennes, serie qrecque, vol. 50.

F. L. Cross, ed., *St. Cyril of Jerusalem's Lectures on the Christian Sacraments,* trans. R. W. Church, London: S.P.C.K., 1951.

J. D. C. Fisher, *Christian Initiation: Baptism in the Medieval West,* London: S.P.C.K., 1965.

Hans Lietzmann, *A History of the Early Church,* trans. B. L. Woolf, 2. vols., New York: World, 1964.

L. L. Mitchell, *Baptismal Anointing*, London: S.P.C.K., 1966.

E. Schillebeeckx, *Christ the Sacrament of the Encounter with God*, trans. P. Barrett *et al*, New York: Sheed and Ward, 1963. Chapters 1 and 2 are especially helpful for an understanding of the paschal mystery of Christ.

J. Strawley, ed., *St. Ambrose on the Sacraments*, trans. T. Thompson, London: S.P.C.K., 1950.

F. Van der Meer, *Augustine the Bishop*, trans. Brian Battershaw and G. R. Lamb, New York: Sheed and Ward, 1961. Chapter 12, "Becoming a Christian" is especially helpful in regard to the ancient practice of baptismal initiation.

E. C. Whitaker, *Documents of the Baptismal Liturgy*, London: S.P.C.K., 1960.

4. PENTECOSTAL EXPERIENCE TODAY

Howard M. Ervin, *These are not Drunken as Ye Suppose*, Plainfield, N. J.: Logos, 1968. An interesting presentation of the baptism in the Holy Spirit as seen from an evangelical Pentecostal standpoint by a Baptist scripture scholar.

Josephine Ford, "Catholic Pentecostalism: New Testament Christianity or Twentieth Century Hysteria," *Jubilee*, June, 1968. Dr. Ford is a member of the theology department of the University of Notre Dame.

Robert Frost, *Aglow With the Spirit*, Northridge, Calif.: Voice, 1965. A dynamic presentation of the reception of the baptism in the Holy Spirit and of the living out of the life of the Spirit by a Protestant layman.

Edward O'Connor, "Pentecost and Catholicism," *The Ecumenist*, July-August, 1968. Father O'Connor is a member of the theology department of the University of Notre Dame and has been involved with the movement there since the spring of 1967.

5. The Gifts and Fruit of the Spirit

Donald Gee, *Concerning Spiritual Gifts,* Springfield, Mo.: Gospel Publishing House: 1937. This book has become a classic of pentecostal theology, reflecting on the gifts of the Spirit from the standpoint of charismatic experience.

John of St. Thomas, *The Gifts of the Holy Ghost,* New York: Sheed and Ward, 1951. Within the scope of the present book we have not found place to adequately discuss the rich theological and spiritual tradition in the Catholic Church on the work of the Holy Spirit. To this end we recommend this and the following book.

B. J. Kelly, *The Seven Gifts,* New York: Sheed and Ward, 1951.

Edward O'Connor, "A Catholic Pentecostal Movement," *Ave Maria,* June 3, 1967.

Karl Rahner, "Charism" and "Prophet," *Theological Dictionary,* New York: Herder and Herder, 1965.

6. Speaking in Tongues

R. H. Gundry, "Ecstatic Utterance," *Journal of Theological Studies,* n.s. 17, Oct. 1966, pp. 299–307.

Henri Nouwen, "A Critical Analysis," *Ave Maria,* June 3, 1967.

Edward O'Connor, "A Catholic Pentecostal Movement," *Ave Maria,* June 3, 1967.

John Sherrill, *They Speak With Other Tongues,* Westwood, N. J.: Spire, 1965, pp. 102–3.

Karl Stern, *The Third Revolution,* Garden City, N. Y.: Doubleday, 1961, pp. 160–7.

David Wilkerson, *The Cross and the Switchblade,* Westwood, N. J.: Spire, 1964, p. 161.

APPENDIX I

Nils Bloch-Hoell, *The Pentecostal Movement,* Oslo: Universitetsforlaget, 1964.

Klaude Kendrick, *The Promise Fulfilled: A History of the Modern Pentecostal Movement,* Springfield, Mo.: Gospel Publishing House, 1961.

John T. Nichol, *Pentecostalism,* New York: Harper and Row, 1966.